PAWS® Presents
COMPUTER KEYBOARDING
2d Edition

Jerry W. Robinson, Ed.D.
T. James Crawford, Ph.D.
Lawrence W. Erickson, Ed.D.
Lee R. Beaumont, Ed.D.

TK30BA
PUBLISHED BY
SOUTH-WESTERN PUBLISHING CO.
CINCINNATI, OH   WEST CHICAGO, IL   DALLAS, TX   LIVERMORE, CA

ISBN: 0–538–60251–1

Library of Congress Catalog Number: 89–61167

Printed in U.S.A.

1 2 3 4 5 6 7 8 9 K 5 4 3 2 1 0 9

CONTRIBUTING AUTHOR

Joyce Rudowski
Member of Computer Department Staff
Cincinnati Country Day School

Ms. Rudowski prepared the Apply-Your-Skill sections
of Lessons 26–34 in Unit 4. For her contributions,
we convey our grateful thanks.

PHOTO CREDITS

Cover: © Marjory Dressler

Page 98: Stock Boston/Gale Zucker

Page 101: Stock Boston/Cary Wolinsky

CONTENTS

PREFACE

People who can operate a computer keyboard with skill have an edge over those who cannot. Pupils who use a keyboard with skill improve their spelling, handwriting, and composing skills. In doing so, they improve their grades in school.

As you learn to key, you will have several partners in learning: your computer, this textbook (PAWS® Presents COMPUTER KEYBOARDING), a diskette (MICROTYPE: The Wonderful World of PAWS®), and your teacher. You, however, are most important because you will determine how well you practice, how much you practice, and the effort with which you practice. These three factors affect the level of skill you will build. If you want to operate a keyboard with skill, you must *intend* to learn, work each day toward a higher goal, and give each practice your best effort.

To key well, you must learn to use the right fingers on the right keys, to make proper motions with the fingers, and to do both without watching your fingers and the keys. Keying without looking is called "touch keyboarding"—your major goal.

To learn to key with skill, you must learn to strike the keys and to operate other parts in the right way. This is called good "technique" (form). Good technique should be your first goal as you learn the reaches to the keys. Good technique will help you to improve finger motions and to save time between motions. Good technique will allow you to key faster than you can now write by hand. Your work will also be easier to read and will have fewer errors.

Good technique requires that the position of the hands and fingers be right because they do the work.

Sit in front of the keyboard so that you can place the fingers in a vertical (upright) position over **ASDF JKL;** (the home keys). The tips of the fingers should just touch the tops of the keys. Move your chair forward or backward or your elbows in or out a bit to place your fingers in this upright position. Do not let your fingers lean over onto one another toward the little fingers.

Curve your fingers deeply like those in the drawing. In this position, the fingers can make quick, direct reaches to the keys and snap back toward the palm of the hand as reaches are completed. A quick-snap stroke is needed for proper keystroking motion.

Place the thumb *lightly* on the space bar, the tip of the right thumb pointing toward the *n* key. Tuck the tip of the left thumb slightly into the palm to keep it out of the way. Strike the space bar with a quick down-and-in motion of the right thumb. Return the thumb quickly to its home position.

TERMS YOU SHOULD KNOW

Disk drive and diskette

Circuit board (including the CPU)

Function keys

ACCURACY degree of freedom from errors (mistakes) measured from zero—usually expressed as 1 error, 2 errors, etc.; sometimes as *errors a minute (eam)*.

BACKSPACE to move the cursor (enter point) to the left one space at a time by striking the left-arrow key once for each character or space.

CPU (central processing unit) the internal operating unit or "brains" of an electronic computer system; *also* "the little black box."

CRT (cathode-ray tube) *see* VDT.

CURSOR a dot or square of light that shows the point on a display screen where the next letter, number, symbol, or space can be entered.

CONTROL the power to cause the hands and fingers to make correct motions; *also* the ability to hold keystroking speed down so that errors (mistakes) are kept to an expected or acceptable number.

CONTROL KEY (CTRL) a special key that when depressed at the same time another key is struck causes that key to perform a special function.

DELETE a key that backspaces and removes copy one character at a time when struck.

DISKETTE (sometimes called DISK) a magnetic, Mylar-coated, record-like disk (encased in a square protective envelope) used for recording, reading, and writing by the CPU (central processing unit).

DISK DRIVE the unit into which a diskette is inserted to be read or written by the CPU (central processing unit).

DISPLAY SCREEN *see* VDT.

DOUBLE-SPACE (DS) verticle line spacing which leaves one blank line space between displayed or printed lines of copy.

EDIT the process of rearranging, changing, and correcting copy; includes proofreading but is not limited to it.

ENTER to input keystrokes; *see* KEY.

ENTER KEY *see* RETURN KEY.

ERROR any misstroke of a key.

ESCAPE KEY (ESC) a key on some computers the use of which lets the operator out of one segment of a program to go to another.

FUNCTION KEYS special keys that when used alone or in combination with other keys perform special functions such as setting margins, centering copy, and so on.

GWAM (gross words a minute) a measure of the rate of keyboarding speed; *GWAM* = total 5-stroke words keyed divided by the time required to key those words.

INDENT to set in from the margin, as the first line of a paragraph.

INSERT to add one or more characters to existing copy.

TERMS YOU SHOULD KNOW, continued

Detached keyboard

Computer printer

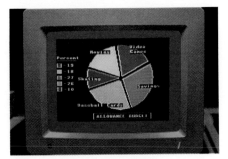

Video display terminal (VDT)

KEY the process of striking keys to record or display words and data.

KEYBOARD an arrangement of keys on a "board" that is attached to or apart from a machine such as a computer; *also* the act of keying.

KEYBOARDING to strike keys to record or display words and data; *also* called keying.

MENU a list of options from which a keyboard operator may (or must) choose in using a word or data processing machine.

MONITOR *see* VDT.

PACE the rate of speed at which keystrokes are made on a keyboard.

PRINT to produce, using a printer, a paper copy of information displayed on a computer screen or stored in computer memory.

PRINTER a unit attached to a computer that produces copy on paper.

PRINT-OUT the printed paper output of a computer.

PROOFREAD to read copy on a display screen or on a print-out against the original source copy and to correct errors (or mark them for correction); *also* one of the steps in editing copy.

RATE the speed of doing a task, as *keying rate*—usually expressed in words a minute or lines per hour.

RETURN to strike the RETURN or ENTER key to cause the cursor (or enter point) to move to the left margin and down to the next line.

RETURN KEY a key that when struck causes the cursor (or enter point) to move to the left margin and down to the next line; *also* ENTER KEY.

SHIFT KEY a key used to make capital letters and certain symbols when struck at the same time as another key.

SHIFT LOCK (CAPS Lock) a key that when depressed causes all letters to be capitalized (ALL-CAPPED).

SINGLE-SPACE (SS) vertical line spacing which leaves no blank space between printed or displayed lines of copy.

SPACE BAR a long bar at the bottom of a keyboard used to move the cursor (enter point) to the right one space at a time.

TAB KEY a key that when struck causes the cursor (enter point) to skip to a preset position as in indenting paragraphs.

TECHNIQUE the degree of skill with which a task is performed; *also* good form, style.

VDT (video display terminal) a TV-like picture tube used to display text (copy) and graphic images.

GET TO KNOW
YOUR COMPUTER

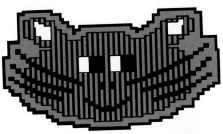

LOCATE ▶

1. Keyboard
2. Display screen (VDT)
3. Disk drive(s)

LOCATE ▶

1. ESC (escape) key
2. Tab key
3. Control key
4. Shift keys
5. CAPS LOCK
6. Option key (Closed Apple)
7. Open Apple
8. Space bar
9. Cursor arrows
10. RETURN key
11. Delete key

Apple® IIe is a trademark of Apple Computer, Inc. Any reference to Apple IIe refers to this footnote.

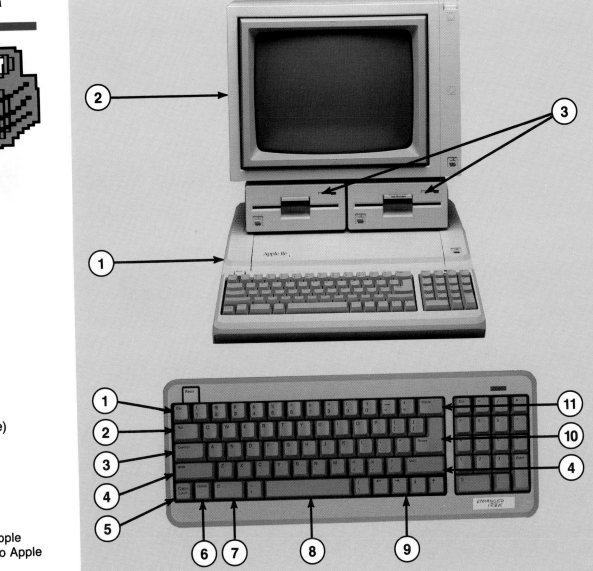

Apple® IIe

GET TO KNOW YOUR COMPUTER

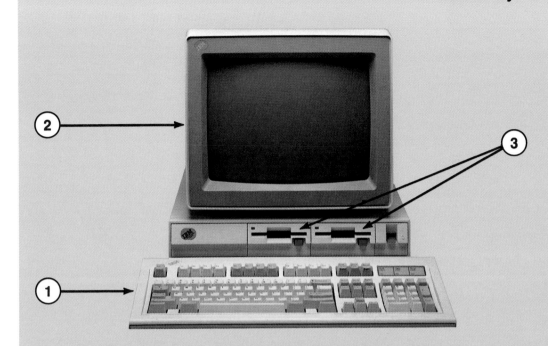

LOCATE ▶

1. Keyboard
2. Display screen (VDT)
3. Disk drive

LOCATE ▶

1. ENTER (return) key
2. Space bar
3. ESC (escape) key
4. Tab key
5. CAPS lock
6. Shift keys
7. Ctrl (control) keys
8. ALT keys
9. Backspace/Delete key
10. Cursor arrows

IBM® PC Standard is a trademark of International Business Machines. Any reference to IBM PC Standard refers to this footnote.

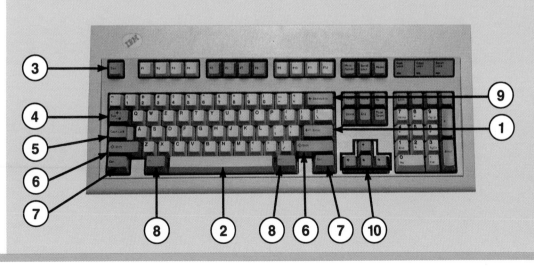

GET TO KNOW YOUR COMPUTER

Tandy 1000

LOCATE ▶

1. Keyboard
2. Display screen (VDT)
3. Disk drive(s)

LOCATE ▶

1. ENTER (return) key
2. Space bar
3. ESC (escape) key
4. Tab key
5. CAPS lock
6. Shift keys
7. CTRL (control) key
8. ALT key
9. Backspace/Delete key
10. Cursor arrows

Tandy® 1000 is a trademark of the Radio Shack Division of Tandy Corporation. Any reference to the Tandy 1000 refers to this footnote.

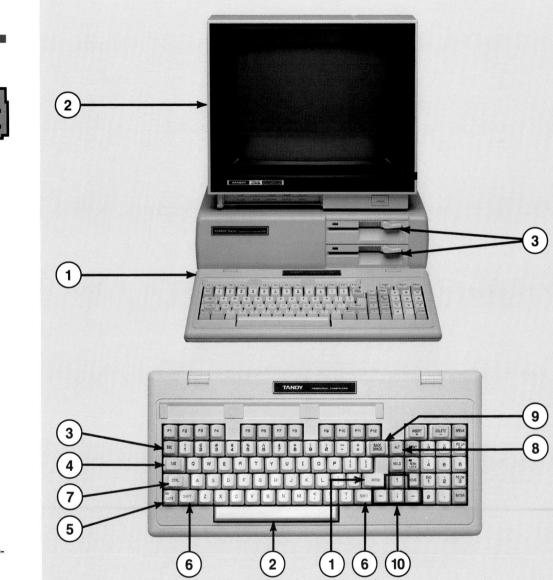

GET READY TO KEY

1. Get to know your computer:

- Apple, page 9
- IBM, page 10
- Tandy, page 11

2. Arrange your work area as shown at the right: ➡

- computer, display screen (or monitor), and disk drives directly in front of your chair
- front edge of keyboard even with front edge of your desk or table
- book at right of computer
- diskette package within easy reach
- unneeded books/supplies moved out of the way

3. Turn on equipment using the ON/OFF switch of the computer/display screen. (Location of ON/OFF switch is different on different models of equipment.) ➡

4. Insert diskette. Follow steps in User's Guide for your computer.

5. Use preset (default) margins and line spacing unless your teacher tells you to set them differently.

Apple

Computer ON/OFF Switch

Monitor ON/OFF Switch

IBM

Computer ON/OFF Switch

Monitor ON/OFF Switch

UNIT 1

YOU LEARN THE LETTER KEYS

Lessons 1-15

YOUR GOALS

In this unit of 15 lessons, you will learn:

1. The keyboard location of each letter key
2. The correct finger to use to strike each key
3. How to strike each key properly (good technique)
4. How to move from key to key quickly and smoothly
5. How to space, shift for capitals, and return
6. How to use basic punctuation keys (;/./,/:/?)

Introduction, Part A

Arrow (Cursor) Keys

1. Read the copy at the right.
2. Study the pictures beneath the copy which show what the arrow keys do.
3. Locate the left/right and up/down arrows in the picture below and then on your own computer keyboard.
4. With your teacher's help, use these keys to move the cursor around the screen.

Introduction, Part B

Backspace/Delete Key

1. Read the copy at the right.
2. Study the pictures below the copy which show the screen before and after the backspace/delete key is used.
3. Find the backspace key on your own keyboard (often at the right end of the number/symbol row of the keyboard).
4. When your teacher directs, use this key to take out (delete) errors you make as you key.

Introduction

A cursor is a light (often blinking) on the screen that shows where the next keystroke will be entered. Arrow keys are used to move the cursor up/down or left/right on the screen to choose items from the menu, to insert copy, or to perform some other task. (The arrow keys are used in some programs to highlight a menu choice.) These four keys often appear as a cluster, usually to the right and below the letter keyboard.

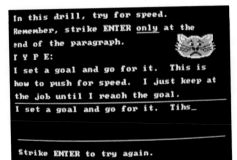

The backspace/delete key lets you backspace and take out (delete) a letter or a series of characters you have already keyed.

Left/Right Arrow Keys

The left-arrow key moves the cursor one space at a time to the left. The right-arrow key moves the cursor one space at a time to the right.

Up/Down Arrow Keys

The up-arrow key moves the cursor up one line at a time. The down-arrow key moves the cursor down one line at a time.

Each time you strike the backspace/delete key, the letter or character to the left of the cursor is taken out (deleted).

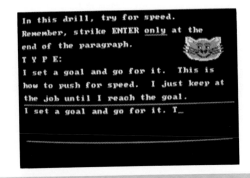

Apply your skill

1. Side margins: 40-space line.
2. Line spacing: DS.
3. Tab stop: 5 spaces.
4. Key the story line for line.

5. Read each sentence and choose from the words in parentheses the one that fits the meaning of the sentence.
6. As you key each sentence, insert (key) the word that correctly completes each sentence.

A FIELD TRIP

Our class took a field trip to the zoo. Our teacher, Miss Meyers, went with us to keep us from getting lost and to make us behave. Mr. Roper drove us there in a school bus.

We saw many animals. My friend Joe thought the zebras were horses, and Lori called the baboon a monkey. We also saw lots of birds. I liked the peafowls best of all, but Ed liked the talking parrots. We saw some snakes, too. Ugh.

After seeing the animals, birds, and reptiles, we had a picnic lunch under a big elm tree and talked about what we had seen. We wanted to stay and play, but Miss Meyers took us back to school.

Think as you key

1 A ____ belongs to the cat family. **(tiger | lizard)**

2 A ____ belongs to the bird family. **(cobra | parakeet)**

3 An ____ belongs to the reptile family. **(iguana | mole)**

4 A ____ belongs to the rodent family. **(rat | shark)**

5 A ____ belongs to the insect family. **(bat | bee)**

6 A ____ belongs to the frog family. **(minnow | tadpole)**

7 A ____ has a pouch to carry its young. **(kangaroo | camel)**

Introduction, Part C

ESC (Escape) Key

1. Read the copy at the right.
2. Study the pictures below the copy which show the change of screen displays when the ESC key is used.
3. Find the ESC key on your own keyboard (usually at the left end of the number/symbol row).
4. When your teacher directs, use this key to move from one part of a computer program to another.

Introduction, Part D

Control (Command) Keys

1. Read the copy at the right.
2. Study the pictures below the copy which show common locations of control (command) keys on computers.
3. Find on your own computer the following keys:

   Apple: control
          open Apple
          closed Apple (option)

   IBM: Ctrl and Alt

   Tandy: CTRL and ALT

The ESC (escape) key permits you to "move around" within a program. For example, if you are working on one part of a lesson, you can strike the ESC key which will take you back to the lesson menu where you can choose another lesson part.

A control (or command) key is used with another key to cause a computer to do a certain task such as print a copy, underline a word, set margins, or set tabs. This key is labeled CTRL.

In addition, a computer may have other command keys that perform special functions. On an Apple these are Open Apple and Closed Apple (or option); on IBM and Tandy, an ALT key.

By striking the ESC key a second time, you may also move from a lesson menu back to the main menu to choose a different lesson. Or, by striking the ESC key again, you can escape from the program and end your practice.

CTRL on an Apple or Tandy 1000 is at the left of the A key. CTRL keys on an IBM are at the left and right of the space bar.

Open Apple and Option keys are left of Apple space bar; Closed Apple, at right of bar.

ALT keys on an IBM are at each end of the space bar; on a Tandy, a single ALT key is at the right of BACKSPACE.

Apple

IBM

Tandy

Lesson 34, Part C

Check keyboarding speed: sentences

1. Key each line twice SS (slowly, then faster); DS below each 2-line group.
2. Take a 1' writing on each of lines 5–8; find *GWAM* on each writing.

All letters used

1 Quaid is to work for a man in town.
2 Zoe may make jell and jam for them.
3 She keeps the dory at the big dock.
4 Livia is to fix the bicycle for me.

5 She is to go to the lake with them.
6 I am to work with them on the sign.
7 Bick is to make a pen for the duck.
8 I shall go for a goal of good form.

1' GWAM | 1 | 2 | 3 | 4 | 5 | 6 | 7 |

Lesson 34, Part D

Check keyboarding speed: paragraphs

1. Take a 1' writing on ¶ 1; find *GWAM*.
2. Take a 1' writing on ¶ 2; find *GWAM*.
3. Take two 2' writings on the ¶s 1 and 2 combined; find *GWAM* on each writing.

To find 2' *GWAM* if you finish ¶ 1 and start ¶ 2:

1. Add 26 to the figure nearest where you stopped.
2. Divide the total by 2.

All letters used | Easy | 1.2 si | 5.1 awl | 90% hfw

Try to keep your eyes on your
book as you key. Just fix them on
each word and let the fingers find
every letter you need for the word.
Have a goal in mind each time
you try a line. Do not quit; keep
on until you make your rate. Size
up each word and key it with vigor.

Lesson 1, Part A

Take keyboarding position

1. Study the picture of correct keyboarding position shown at the right.
2. Take good position directly in front of the keyboard. As you do so, follow each step listed at the right of the picture.

LESSON 1

Position points

1. Sit back in chair; back straight; lean a bit forward from your hips.
2. Place both feet on the floor (if possible) for body balance.
3. Place your hands over the middle row of letter keys—left index finger on **F**, right index finger on **J**.
4. Keep fingers well curved, the wrists low.

Desks or tables and chairs should be adjusted for proper height.

Lesson 1, Part B

Place your fingers in home-key position

1. Find on the chart the letters **A S D F** (home keys for left hand).
2. Using your left hand, place
   index finger on **F**
   middle finger on **D**
   ring finger on **S**
   little finger on **A**
   on your computer keyboard.
3. Find on the chart the letters **J K L ;** (semicolon). These are the home keys for the right hand.
4. Starting with your index finger, place the fingers of your right hand on **J K L ;**
5. Place the right thumb lightly on the space bar.

Lesson 34, Part A

Keyboard review and mastery

Key each set of 3 lines twice (slowly, then faster) to recall reaches to all letters and figures.

All letters used

1 Jacki gave us a new quilt she made.
2 Toby will fix his bike on the pier.
3 Zoe paid the old man for the fruit.

All figures used

4 There are 26 letters and 10 digits.
5 Of the 17 pupils, only 2 were late.
6 Jon lives at 3849 West 15th Street.

Lesson 34, Part B

Check keyboarding technique

As you key the lines, have your teacher check to see if you:

1. keep your fingers well curved
2. keep your fingers upright (not leaning over onto your little fingers)
3. keep your hands quiet (almost motionless)
4. strike each key with a fast-snap stroke and release it quickly
5. keep your eyes on the copy at the right.

All letters used

1 It is up to me to set the new goal.
2 I am to ski on the lake by the inn.
3 Alex has left for the pier to fish.
4 Ask the boy how to get to the pool.
5 Lori may see a lion cub at the zoo.
6 Are we to mow the field by the gym?
7 Verna will sing a solo in the show.
8 Quin said to meet him at the plaza.
9 Jane had a cone of peach ice cream.
10 Five girls will plan the big party.

Lesson 1, Part C

Learn to strike home keys and space bar

1. Study at the right the description and drawings of how to strike a key.
2. Study at the right the description and drawings of how to strike the space bar.
3. Curve your fingers and place them lightly on the home keys:

   left fingers on **ASDF**
   right fingers on **JKL;**

   and the right thumb lightly on the space bar.
4. Practice (key) twice each of the lines shown below the keyboard chart.

To end one line and start the next one:

Reach to the right with the little finger of the right hand and strike the RETURN or ENTER key. Doing this will move the cursor (enter point) to the beginning of the next line down.

Keystroking technique

Strike the key with a quick, sharp tap of the finger. Snap the tip of the finger slightly toward the palm of the hand as the keystroke is completed.

Spacing technique

Strike the space bar with the thumb of the right hand. Use a quick down-and-in motion (toward the palm of the hand).

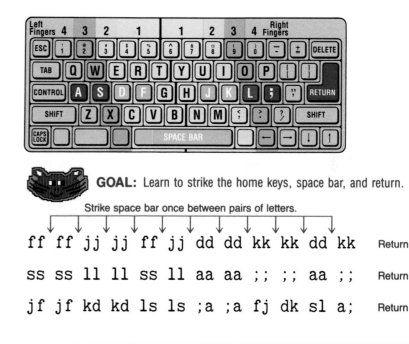

GOAL: Learn to strike the home keys, space bar, and return.

Strike space bar once between pairs of letters.

```
ff ff jj jj ff jj dd dd kk kk dd kk    Return

ss ss ll ll ss ll aa aa ;; ;; aa ;;    Return

jf jf kd kd ls ls ;a ;a fj dk sl a;    Return
```

Apply your skill

1. Side margins: 40-space line.
2. Line spacing: DS.
3. Tab stop: 5 spaces.
4. Key the story line for line.

5. Read the sentences at the right.
6. As you key each sentence, insert (key) the word or words about your friends to complete the sentence.

FORT JIM OR FORT DAVID

David and Jim were best friends who played together every day. Sometimes they played at Jim's house and sometimes at David's. Once in a while they argued about where they were going to play.

One day at Jim's house they built a fort in the backyard. They built it of wood, blankets, and rope. The fort was so big that they could stand on it. It had a high wall to protect them in case any animals came by.

They asked their parents if they could sleep in the fort. After dinner Jim and David went out to the fort to spend the night. They took blankets, pillows, comic books, and a flashlight. David wanted to call the fort Fort David, but Jim wanted to call it Fort Jim. Finally they decided to call it Fort D. J.

Think as you key

1 My best friend's name is _____.
2 We like to _____ when we are together.
3 One time we went to the _____ together.
4 _____ and _____ are also my friends.
5 If I could pick anyone in the world to be my friend, I would pick _____

Practice
home-key letters

1. Key each line once as shown. If you forget the location of a key, find it on the chart; *do not* look at your keyboard.
2. If time permits, key the lines again. Try to strike the keys at a faster speed.

GOAL: Curved fingers; quick-snap keystrokes

Space once for each blank space.

1	f ff j jj d dd k kk s ss l ll a aa; Return
2	j f jf k d kd l s ls ; a ;a ;a fja; Return
3	jk fd kl ds l; sa fj dk sl a; fj a; Return
4	sa jk ds lk df kj sa kl fd jk a; fj Return

GOAL: To improve keystroking and spacing

Space after ; and between words.

1	a a ad ad lad lad a a as as ask ask Return
2	ad ad as as jak jak ask ask fad fad Return
3	a jak; ask all; all ads; ask a lad; Return
4	as all; a fad; ask dad; ask a lass; Return

Lesson 33, Part C

Check keyboarding speed: sentences

1. Key each line twice SS (slowly, then faster); DS below each 2-line group.
2. Take a 1' writing on each of lines 5–8; find *GWAM* on each writing.

All letters used

1 Robby saw a large squid in the net.
2 Zuma packed five jars of wax beans.
3 Leo, keep your fingers well curved.
4 Tina had squab; Ray had roast duck.

5 Nicole kept the ivy in a clay bowl.
6 Rico is to fix the bus sign for us.
7 Mela paid for the six bars of soap.
8 Andy is to visit the city map firm.

1' GWAM | 1 | 2 | 3 | 4 | 5 | 6 | 7 |

Lesson 33, Part D

Check keyboarding speed: paragraphs

1. Take a 1' writing on ¶ 1; find *GWAM*.
2. Take a 2' writing on ¶ 2; find *GWAM*.
3. Take two 2' writings on the ¶s 1–2 combined; find *GWAM*.

To find 2' *GWAM* if you finish ¶ 1 and start ¶ 2:

1. Add 26 to the figure nearest where you stopped.
2. Divide the total by 2

All letters used | Easy | 1.2 si | 4.6 awl | 90% hfw

As I explore a new speed zone,
I try my best to control each move.
A major goal is to make every move
quickly and in the right way.

If I lower my speed, I can pay
more attention to my work patterns.
If I drop the rate about two words,
I get new control and cut mistakes.

Lesson 2, Part A

Get ready to key

1. Get ready to key as directed on page 12 or as directed by your teacher.
2. Arrange your work area as directed on page 12.
3. Take keyboarding position as shown on page 16.

Lesson 2, Part B

Review home keys

1. Curve your fingers and place them on the home keys:

    left   right

    ASDF JKL;

2. Key each line shown at the right.
3. If time permits, key the lines again at a faster speed.

RECALL ▼

- Strike the space bar once after a letter standing alone, after groups of letters, and between words.
- Strike RETURN or ENTER at the end of a line to move the cursor (enter point) to the beginning of the next line down.

LESSON 2

Plan for learning new keys

1. Find the new key on the keyboard chart.
2. *Look* at your keyboard. Find the new key on it.
3. Study the reach-technique drawing at the left of the practice lines (see page 20).
4. Learn which finger strikes the key. (Look at the reach-technique drawing for the new key.)
5. Curve your fingers; place them in home-key position.
6. *Watch your finger* as you reach it to the new key and back to home position a few times. (Try to keep it curved as you reach.)
7. Practice twice each of the 3 lines at the right of the reach-technique drawing:
    slowly, to learn the new reach;
    faster, to improve keystroking.
8. If time permits, practice each line again.

Strike the space bar once.

1 jj ff kk dd ll ss ;; aa fj a; fj a;   Return

2 a; sl dk fj jf kd ls ;a ds kl fd jk   Return

3 as as ad ad jak jak all all fad fad   Return

4 a jak; as all; a sad lad; a fall ad   Return

Lesson 33, Part A

Keyboard review and mastery

Key each set of 3 lines twice (first slowly, then faster) to recall reaches to all letters and figures.

Lesson 33, Part B

Check keyboarding technique

As you key the lines, have your teacher check to see if you:

1. keep your fingers well curved
2. keep your fingers upright (not leaning over onto your little fingers)
3. keep your hands quiet (almost motionless)
4. strike each key with a fast-snap stroke and release it quickly
5. keep up a steady pace

All letters used

1 Ryan keeps a frog in his fish tank.
2 Dixie is just as quick as Willa is.
3 Buzz may have taken a silver medal.

All figures used

4 Alexis is to be 13 on September 26.
5 Buck weighs 105 pounds; Angus, 108.
6 Of the 495 pupils, 107 were absent.

All letters used

1 Peg swam in all events at the meet.
2 Denzil makes a golf shot look easy.
3 They saw the jet zoom into the sky.
4 All is quiet just before the storm.
5 The man in the moon is an old myth.
6 The big clock chimed loudly at six.
7 Flo should win the next two events.
8 Leon said he may join the ski club.
9 Does she toot the bugle with vigor?

Lesson 2, Part C

Learn new keys: H and E

For each key to be learned in this lesson and the lessons that follow, use the "Plan for learning new keys" given on page 19.

1. Study the plan with your teacher's help. Follow the steps in the plan to learn correct reaches to **h** and **e**.

2. Key each set of 3 lines twice: once slowly; again, faster.

Reach technique for h

Reach to *left* with *right first* finger.

Reach technique for e

Reach *up* with *left second* finger.

Learn h

1   j hj hj ah ah ha ha had had has has   Return

2   h hj hj ha ha ah ah hah hah had had   Return

3   ah ha; ha ha; has had; has ash; hah   Return

Learn e

4   d e ed ed el el eke eke led led eel   Return

5   ed ed el el lee lee led led elf elf   Return

6   a lake; a jade; a leek; a jade sale   Return

Combine h and e

7   eh eh he he she she held held sheds   Return

8   he had; she has; a shed; he has ash   Return

9   a half; a jade; she led; he had ale   Return

Apply your skill

1. Side margins: 40-space line.
2. Line spacing: DS.
3. Tab stop: 5 spaces.
4. Key the story line for line.

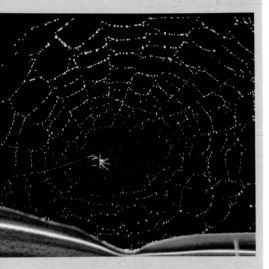

5. Read the poem at the right.
6. As you key each sentence, insert (key) a word that rhymes with the last word of the line above it. Read the bold words below the poems for some rhyming ideas.

MY FAVORITE PET

Once I had a pet spider. Her name was Madeline. She lived in a small glass castle in my room. She spun a web of gold. I rolled the gold thread into a ball each morning.

One day Madeline stood on top of her castle and started to spin. She spun and spun gold thread. Soon the whole castle was covered with thread. But Madeline did not stop spinning.

That night the case was solid gold. Madeline was gone. She had locked herself inside the castle of gold. Many days later the castle was dark. I looked very closely and saw that it was covered with baby spiders.

Think as you key

1 Sammy had a big black cat
2 Who lived inside an old black _____.
3 When Sammy went to school each day,
4 His big black cat went out to _____.
5 When Sammy came back home from school
6 He found his cat sitting on a _____.

hat | mat | play | sleigh | stool | mule

Lesson 2, Part D

Improve keystroking technique

1. Key each set of 3 lines twice: once slowly, once more at a faster speed.
2. As time permits, key the lines again.

 TECHNIQUE GOAL ▶

- Fingers curved and upright (straight up and down over home keys)

 TECHNIQUE GOAL ▶

- Keystrokes quick and snappy

Color verticals (not to be keyed) divide the lines into phrases.

TECHNIQUE GOAL ▶

- Space quickly and smoothly between words
- Make returns without stopping at ends of lines

Practice words   R = Return

1 hj ed ah ah he he led led heed heed   R

2 a ha he el eel led had she hah hall   R

3 ah el he ha elf she led hah eel fed   R

Practice phrases (word groups)

4 a lake | a hall | a sled | a shed | as half   R

5 he had | as she | she led | a jade | a desk   R

6 he has | she fed | ask a lad | a jak fell   R

Practice key words

7 a as he she has had ask led all add   R

8 he see sea seek lake half jell fall   R

9 he fed all; has a lake; he had jell   R

Lesson 32, Part C

Improve keyboarding speed: sentences

1. Key each line twice SS at your best speed.
2. Take a 1' writing on each of lines 6–9; find *GWAM* on each writing.

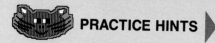 **PRACTICE HINTS** ▶

- quiet hands and arms
- quick, sharp keystrokes
- brisk, steady pace

All letters used

1 Be quick to return at line endings.
2 Quin has used a quote in his paper.
3 Liz turned on a quick kick and won.
4 The ball curved into the sand trap.
5 Marj has yet to reach fourth place.
6 Eddy took a lead at the sixth hole.
7 Five or six boys had left the camp.
8 Vic took the quiz and left it here.
9 To make a goal is to grow in skill.

1' GWAM | 1 | 2 | 3 | 4 | 5 | 6 | 7 |

Lesson 32, Part D

Improve keyboarding speed: paragraph

1. Take two 1' writings on the easy ¶ for speed; find *GWAM* on each.
2. Take two 2' writings on the ¶ for speed; find *GWAM* on each.

1' *GWAM* = nearest figure above where you stopped.

2' *GWAM* = 1' *GWAM* ÷ 2

All letters used | Easy | 1.2 si | 5.1 awl | 90% hfw

If you think the word you want
to key, the fingers will know what
they are to do. Just relax, then,
and let them go. Try not to pause
after you strike a key. Quickly
move on to the next one. Be sure to
size up each word and then key it.

Learn new keys: I and R

1. Learn the location of new keys
i and r by following the steps
in the "Plan for learning new
keys" on page 19.
2. Key each set of 3 lines twice:
once slowly, again at a faster
speed.

Reach technique for i

Reach *up* with *right second* finger.

Reach technique for r

Reach *up* with *left first* finger.

LESSON 3

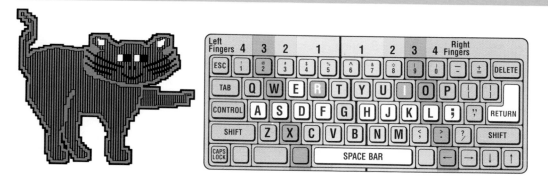

Learn i

1   k i ik ik is is if if hi hi did did   Return

2   i ik ik if if is is kid kid aid aid   R

3   if he; a kid; a lie; he did; she is   R

Learn r

4   f r rf rf jar jar ark ark jerk jerk   R

5   r rf rf jar jar her her are are ark   R

6   a jar; a rake; a lark; her red jar;   R

Combine i and r

7   sir sir air air rid rid ire ire irk   R

8   is rid; is red; his ire; a fir fire   R

9   is hers; his red hair; a fair ride;   R

Lesson 32, Part A

**Keyboard review
and mastery**

1. Key each line twice SS: once slowly, then faster. DS below each 2-line group.
2. Take a 1' writing on line 3; find *GWAM*.

All letters used

1 jack size flex stop very such equal
2 by me to own if she too big did pay
3 Roz read a dial on the pump for me.

1' GWAM | 1 | 2 | 3 | 4 | 5 | 6 | 7 |

Lesson 32, Part B

Improve keystroking technique

1. Key each line twice SS: once slowly, then faster. DS below each 2-line group.
2. Take a 1' writing on line 10; find *GWAM*.

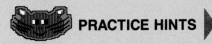 **PRACTICE HINTS** ▶

- curved, upright fingers
- quiet hands and arms
- quick, sharp keystrokes
- brisk, steady pace

Adjacent-key combinations (side by side)

1 are pop her buy try ask pod bop pew
2 a ewe│we opt│we owe│ask her│has ore
3 Sophie said her dad was very pious.

Long, direct reaches with same finger

4 my ice any curb nice mush rice cent
5 the sun│for ice│any fun│is my niece
6 Lyn set a nice pace on the gym ice.

Outside reaches (third and fourth fingers)

7 as pow zap lax has sap wan sow flax
8 all saw│lax law│has flax│a pop quiz
9 Lowan said all can pass a pop quiz.

Easy sentence (balanced-hand words)

10 Al cut down the shrub for the girl.

1' GWAM | 1 | 2 | 3 | 4 | 5 | 6 | 7 |

Improve keystroking technique

1. Key each set of 3 lines twice: once slowly, once more at a faster speed.
2. If time permits, key each set of lines again.

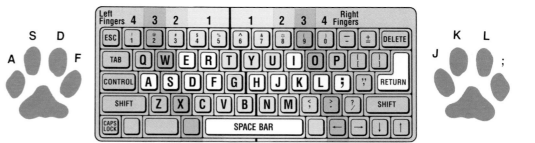

 TECHNIQUE GOAL ▶

- Reach with one finger at a time; keep other fingers over their home keys.

 TECHNIQUE GOAL ▶

- Space quickly between the words of each phrase.

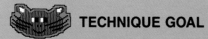 **TECHNIQUE GOAL** ▶

- Keep the cursor moving steadily, word by word.

Practice words

1 el led is sir if fir ik ski re jeer   Return

2 he is el as ha re if ah fir she led   R

3 air die sir hid ski ark jar eke all   R

Practice phrases (word groups)

4 ah ha|he is|if she|he did|if he did   R

5 as is|he has|is his|she led|ask her   R

6 she did|her jar|all kids|if she did   R

Practice key words

7 a ah ha he if is as she did all jak   R

8 air jar fir has ask had led her aid   R

9 is fir; he led; if a kid; has a jar   R

Apply your skill

1. Side margins: 40-space line.
2. Line spacing: DS.
3. Tab stop: 5 spaces.
4. Key the story line for line.

5. Think about the riddles in the story you just keyed.
6. Make up your own riddles by choosing words to complete the clues in lines 1, 3, and 5.
7. As you key the sentences, insert your chosen clue words in lines 1, 3, and 5. Add the word that completes the clue when keying lines 2, 4, and 6.

RIDDLES

What is taller than a house? Lots of things. What is taller than a house and grows in the woods? Lots of trees. What grows in the woods of California? Maybe the redwood trees that stand tall and straight in the redwood forests.

What is bigger than a toad? Lots of things. What is bigger than a toad and lives in a tree? Lots of animals. What lives in a tree and buries nuts in the ground? Maybe a squirrel. Is it a gray squirrel or a red squirrel?

What is smaller than your hand? Lots of things. What is smaller than your hand and lives in a pond? Lots of animals. What lives in a pond and grows up to live out of water? Maybe a pollywog or tadpole. It may become a frog or a toad when it grows up.

Think as you key

1 What is smaller than a _____?
2 It could be a _____ .
3 What is green and bigger than a _____?
4 It could be a _____ .
5 What sleeps during the day and has _____?
6 It could be a _____ .

Review what you have learned

1. Review the steps for getting ready to keyboard (page 12).
2. Review the points for arranging your work area (page 12).
3. Take good keyboarding position (see below).
4. Key each set of 3 lines twice: first at an easy pace, then at a faster speed.

Good keyboarding position

REVIEW A

Home-row emphasis (Keep unused fingers on home keys.)

1 a;sldkfj a;sldkfj fdsajkl; fdsajkl;   Return

2 as ask sad lad had all fad jak fall   R

3 all lads had hash; a lass had a jak   R

Third-row emphasis (*Reach* up without moving the hands.)

4 ed ik ed ik rf de ik fr ded kik frf   R

5 if he is eh re fir she did die rake   R

6 he led her; he has fir; a jade jar;   R

All keystrokes learned (Quick down-and-in spacing.)

7 lad she jak had rid sir her all aid   R

8 fall jade heir jerk rise hail shall   R

9 ask her; a jade fish; his jell jar;   R

Lesson 31, Part C

Improve keyboarding response patterns

1. Key each line twice SS: once slowly, then faster. DS below each 2-line group.
2. Take two 1' writings on line 9; find *GWAM* on each writing.

 **GOALS**

- lines 1–3 slowly, letter by letter
- lines 4–6 quickly, word by word
- lines 7–9, change speed to fit difficulty of word

Letter response

```
1  add ill act ink age hop are inn ate
2  saw you get ink add oil mom was ill
3  Kim was ill after you saw him jump.
```

Word response

```
4  ant ivy ape jay cub pal elf rob hay
5  to sow is due an owl of six the wig
6  The tug may tow us to the big dock.
```

Combination response

```
7  lip dug ear lap tab nap tea yap wet
8  rob him bit you may wax row for him
9  We may eat eggs and ham at the inn.
```

1' GWAM | 1 | 2 | 3 | 4 | 5 | 6 | 7 |

Lesson 31, Part D

Improve keyboarding speed

1. Take two 1' timed writings on the ¶; find *GWAM* on each.
2. Take two 2' timed writings on the ¶; find *GWAM* on each.

1' *GWAM* = nearest figure above where you stopped.

2' *GWAM* = 1' *GWAM* ÷ 2

| All letters used | Easy | 1.2 si | 5.1 awl | 90% hfw |

```
            .       2       .       4       .       6
     Sit back now and then to size
     .       8       .      10       .      12
up just how you key.  Do you curve
     14       .      16       .      18       .
each finger and keep it low?  Do
   20       .      22       .      24       .      26
you snap the tip quickly toward the
     .      28       .      30       .      32       .      34
hand?  If not, be sure to give such
     .      36       .      38       .      40       .
items major effort next.  It pays.
```

Review A, Part 2

Improve keystroking speed by repeating words

Each word in each line is shown twice. Key a word the first time at an easy speed; repeat it at a faster speed.

1. Key each line once; use the plan suggested above.
2. Key the lines again; try to keep the cursor moving steadily.

Review A, Part 3

Improve keystroking speed by repeating phrases

1. Key each phrase twice as shown. Speed up the second try on the phrase.
2. Key the lines again to improve your speed.

Review A, Part 4

Build steady cursor movement

1. Key each line. Keep the cursor moving steadily.
2. Key each line again. Try to finish each line without slowing down or stopping.

 GOAL: To speed up the combining of letters

```
1   is is|sir sir|he he|her her|his his      Return

2   re re|ire ire|if if|fir fir|are are

3   he he|she she|hi hi|hid hid|jar jar
```

 GOAL: To speed up spacing between words

```
1   ah ha ah ha|if he if he|as if as if      Return

2   if a if a|as he as he|if she if she

3   he has jade jars; he has jade jars;
```

 GOAL: To keep cursor moving steadily

```
1   he said he had a jade sale all fall       Return

2   she said she reads all ads she sees

3   she also said his fir desks irk her
```

Lesson 31, Part A

Keyboard review and mastery

Key each line twice SS: once slowly, again at a faster speed. DS below each 2-line group.

All letters/figures used

1 lag 915 hue 673 fix 482 cup 370 jak
2 6 doz.|150 lbs.|248 ft.|379 sq. in.
3 I was born May 26, 1980, in Denver.

Lesson 31, Part B

Improve keyboarding technique

1. Key lines 1–6 twice SS: once slowly, then faster. DS below each 2-line group.

 **GOALS**

- down-and-in spacing
- out-and-down shifting
- no pause before or after returning

2. Key lines 7–12 once DS at an easy pace; then key the lines again faster.

Space bar

1 an am by in buy ham boy pen may pen
2 an inn|any of|by the|in all|if they
3 Ann won a big urn at the city fair.

Shift keys and LOCK

4 Mary and Don are at the Yacht Club.
5 Ms. Epps is going to Madrid, Spain.
6 Did you watch STAR TREK on Tuesday?

Return

7 Do not slow down
8 at the line ending.
9 Reach out quickly with
10 the little finger and tap
11 the return. Then begin the
12 new copy line without a pause.

Learn new keys: O and T

1. Learn the location of new keys o and t by following the steps in the "Plan for learning new keys" on page 19.
2. Key each set of 3 lines twice: once slowly, again at a faster speed.

Reach technique for o

Reach *up* with *right third* finger.

Reach technique for t

Reach *up* with *left first* finger.

LESSON 4

Learn O

1 l o ol ol do do so so of of old old   Return

2 o o ol ol or or for for oak oak off

3 do so; a doe; a foe; of all; of oak

Learn t

4 f t t tf tf it it at at the the tie

5 t tf tf ft ft it it sit sit fit fit

6 if it; it is; a fit; it fit; tie it

Combine O and t

7 too too lot lot toe toe dot dot hot

8 to do; is to; if so; is hot; to jot

9 of it; do it; a lot; to rot; dot it

Apply your skill

1. Side margins: 40-space line.
2. Line spacing: DS.
3. Tab stop: 5 spaces.
4. Key the story line for line.

5. Read the lists of words shown at the right. Notice that one letter in each row is followed by a blank space. Think of a word beginning with that letter.
6. Key each row of words. Insert your chosen words where there is only a first letter.

JUST J

John, Jean, Jerry, and Joan ran to the jungle gym. Joan swung on the bottom railing. Jerry climbed to the highest part. John just ran around at the bottom. A sandbox was near the jungle gym. Jean jumped into into the sandbox.

Joan left the jungle gym and joined Jean in the sandbox. They built a castle in the sand and called it the Jolly Time castle. It had a giant flag on top. The flag was just a bandana that Jean brought from home.

John and Jerry jumped off the jungle gym. They joined Jean and Joan in the sand. They built two new rooms onto the castle. All pretended that they lived in the castle. Jean, Joan, Jerry, and John enjoyed their day at the park.

Think as you key

1 apple bear c_____ delightful elephant
2 f_____ giant hickory Indian jungle kayak
3 lion monkey n_____ onion pickle queen
4 rooster s_____ tunnel upside violet
5 wonderful Xerox yellow z_____

Improve keyboarding technique

1. Key each set of 3 lines twice: once slowly, once more at a faster speed.
2. If time permits, key each set of lines again.

 TECHNIQUE GOAL ▶

- Reach with one finger at a time; keep other fingers over their home keys.

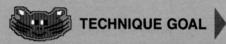 **TECHNIQUE GOAL** ▶

- Space quickly between the words of each phrase.

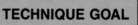 **TECHNIQUE GOAL** ▶

- Keep the cursor moving steadily, word by word.

Practice words

```
1  if to so at is do ad of or ad he as    Return

2  all she toe ask jet for dot kit did

3  fish jade lake hero this fort flake
```

Practice phrases (word groups)

```
4  if so|it is|to do|if it is|to do so

5  he did it|if the doe|she took a jet

6  is for all|for the lot|she is a hit
```

Practice key words

```
7  or as he of it do is to if so at ad

8  for the all old are ask fit she did

9  ask for the jar; all are at the jet
```

Lesson 30, Part B

**Review the figure keys
and commonly used symbols**

Key each line twice SS: once slowly,
again at a faster speed. DS below
each 2-line group.

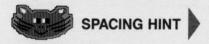 **SPACING HINT** ▶

- When : is used to state time, no
  space follows it.

All figures used

1 We sold 7 elms, 10 ash, and 45 oak.

2 The sum of 53, 209, and 416 is 678.

3 I read pages 30–38, reviewed 16–29.

4 Gus said, "I have a 10–speed bike."

5 Don't stop now; go for a big prize.

6 Shep, can't you key one half (1/2)?

7 Han Song–Ki has a cafe at 746 Main.

8 Ana left at 8:15 a.m. for San Juan.

Lesson 30, Part C

Improve keyboarding speed

1. Take two 1' writings on the ¶ for
   speed; find *GWAM* on each.
2. Take two 2' writings on the ¶ for
   speed; find *GWAM* on each.

1' *GWAM* = nearest figure above
where you stopped.

2' *GWAM* = 1' *GWAM* ÷ 2

Paragraph timed writing

All letters used	Easy	1.2 si	5.1 awl	90% hfw

Win as if you are used to it,
and lose just as though you like it
for a change. In this way you show
that you are quite as big when you
lose the prize as when you take it.
The next time you make a goal, act
just as if you are very used to it.

Learn new keys: N and G

1. Learn the location of new keys **n** and **g** by following the standard plan (see page 19).
2. Key each set of 3 lines twice: once slowly, again at a faster speed.

Reach technique for n

Reach *down* with *right first* finger.

Reach technique for g

Reach to *right* with *left first* finger.

LESSON 5

Learn n

1   j n nj nj an an and and ant ant end   Return

2   n n nj nj an an in in no no end end

3   an end; an oak; and do; on the land

Learn g

4   f g gf gf go go fog fog dog dog got

5   g g gf gf go go got got dig dig log

6   a dog; a log; to go; he got; to jog

Combine n and g

7   on an in go ago and got end gin nag

8   to dig; in fog; go into; to sign in

9   go on; sign in; long ago; good sign

Keyboard review and mastery

Key each pair of lines once SS at an easy, steady pace; DS below each 2-line group. As time permits, key again lines that were difficult for you.

LESSON 30

All letters used

h/u	1	hush bush lush push rush such hauls
	2	Quig hauled the lush shrub for you.
i/v	3	via vie vim vis live view jive visa
	4	Livia is to view the villa at five.
j/w	5	wow jaw win jut bow just jowl major
	6	Jewel just won a major jump or two.
k/x	7	ask six kit mix kick flax bike flex
	8	Alex took the six bike kits to Lex.
l/y	9	lay lye fly sly ply rely lays style
	10	Elly is to fly in style to a rally.
m/z	11	am ham zam zoo zoom maze ooze amaze
	12	Mazy just amazed my mom at the zoo.

Lesson 5, Part B

Improve keystroking speed

1. Key each set of 3 lines twice: once slowly, once more at a faster speed.
2. If time permits, key each set of lines again.

TECHNIQUE GOAL ▶

- Reach finger to its target key; keep the hands in place over the home keys.

TECHNIQUE GOAL ▶

- Space quickly between words; use a down-and-in motion of the right thumb.

TECHNIQUE GOAL ▶

- Speed up between letters within words; space quickly between words.

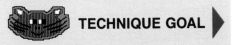

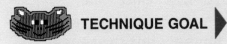

Practice words

1 if or do is go an to ha oak eel fog   Return

2 all the and did for fog end ask jig

3 land hang then frog than golf their

Practice phrases

4 if so|to go|it is|do it|is on|of an

5 if she|is for|to end|to jog|for the

6 and go|in a fog|on a log|an old dog

Practice key words

7 the for got and did she fit off kit

8 aid end all ask old jet led jog are

9 lend disk glen torn jell flag thank

Apply your skill

1. Side margins: 40-space line.
2. Line spacing: DS.
3. Tab stop: 5 spaces.
4. Key the story line for line.

5. Read each think-as-you-key statement at the right.
6. As you key each sentence, insert (key) in the blank the word from the story that correctly completes each sentence.

EVA'S TRIP

Eva wanted to go out west. She read stories about the Indians who lived there. She wanted to see the desert. Most of all she wanted to meet an Indian. Eva thought that Indians lived in tents called tepees.

One summer Eva went to New Mexico to visit her cousin Julie. She saw the flat, sandy desert. She met a friend of Julie's named Sarah. Eva liked Sarah, and Sarah liked Eva. They played together every day. Some days they played at Sarah's house.

Eva told Sarah that she wanted to meet a real Indian. Sarah told Eva that she already knew a real Indian. Sarah was an Indian. She lived in a house, not a tepee. Sarah was much like Eva.

Think as you key

1 Eva read stories about _____ .

2 She learned that some lived in the _____ .

3 Eva went to New Mexico to see her _____ .

4 She became friends with an _____ girl.

5 Her new friend lived in a _____ .

Learn new keys: left shift key and . (period)

1. Learn the location of new keys **left shift** and **. (period)** by following the standard plan (see page 19).
2. Key each set of 3 lines twice: once slowly, again at a faster speed.

Control of left shift key

Reach *down* with *left little* finger; shift, strike, release.

Reach technique for . (period)

Reach *down* with *right third* finger; space twice after. at end of sentence.

NOTE: Space **once** at the end of an abbreviated word and after periods following first letters of names (initials). Space **twice** after a period at the end of a sentence.

LESSON 6

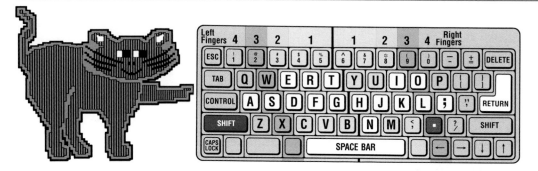

Learn left shift key

1 Ja Ja Na Na Hal Hal Kae Kae Jae Jae   Return

2 Kae fell; Hal has jade; Jane got it

3 I see Hal is to aid Jan at Oak Lake

Learn . (period)

4 l . . .l .l ed. ed. ft. ft. in. in.

5 . .l .l ea. ea. fl. fl. rd. rd. gr.

6 fl. hr. rd. ea. fed. gal. i.e. e.g.

Combine left shift key and .

7 I do. I did. Jae is. Ike has it.

8 I see. Nan said it. Hal has gold.

9 Ned has a kite. Ida lost her skis.

Lesson 29, Part B

Review the figure keys

Key each line twice SS: once slowly, again at a faster speed. DS below each 2-line group.

Lesson 29, Part C

Build keyboarding speed

1. Take two 15″ writings on each line. If you finish before time is called, start over. *GWAM* is shown word by word.

 **GOAL** ▶

- To finish keying the line just as time is called.

2. Take two 1′ writings on the ¶. See how many words you can key in a minute.
3. If time permits, key a 2′ writing on the ¶ (2′ *GWAM* = 1′ *GWAM* divided by 2).

All figures used

1 Maria got 38 of the 40 items right.
2 Ms. Han has 10 pens and 26 pencils.
3 Ty jogged 5 miles; then he rode 17.
4 We sold 385 chances; they sold 290.
5 Team 3 has 571 points; Team 4, 629.

Sentence timed writing

15″ GWAM

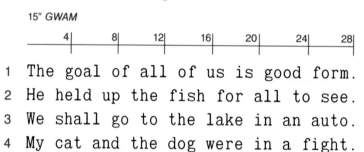

1 The goal of all of us is good form.
2 He held up the fish for all to see.
3 We shall go to the lake in an auto.
4 My cat and the dog were in a fight.

Paragraph timed writing

| All letters used | Easy | 1.2 si | 5.1 awl | 90% hfw |

You will learn to key well if you just do your best each day. A quick and exact stroke to each key is what you need to get to the top prize. Try to move with speed now.

Improve keystroking technique

1. Key each set of 3 lines twice: once slowly, once more at a faster speed.
2. If time permits, key each set of lines again.

Space once:

- after ;
- after . used with abbreviations and initials

Space twice:

- after . at the end of a sentence except at the end of a line; there, return without spacing.

 **TECHNIQUE GOAL** ▶

- Space quickly between words; do not stop between them.

Practice abbreviations and initials

1 Lela has a sled; she lets Nan ride.   Return

2 He said rd. for road; ft. for feet.

3 Lt. Nagle let K. L. take her skiff.

Practice sentences

4 I like Nan a lot. I also like Jae.

5 Lara is in Haiti. Kae is in Lagos.

6 Ian had an egg dish; Ina took hash.

Practice key words

7 or he to if go is of it of an el so

8 and for she got old led off ask jet

9 Kala said she got a fine jade ring.

Keyboard review and mastery

Key each pair of lines once SS at an easy, steady pace; DS below each 2-line group. As time permits, key again lines that were difficult for you.

LESSON 29

All letters used

a/n	1	a an and land hand snap gnat snacks
	2	Zane has lent a hand to an old man.
b/o	3	box boy lob job boat oboe book robe
	4	The boy took the box to a big boat.
c/p	5	pac cup cap cop cape cope pick pack
	6	Pack the cups the cops have picked.
d/q	7	due quit duty quiz dual squad squid
	8	Quade did quit their squad quickly.
e/r	9	re red her are here hire jerk there
	10	Erica wore a red dress to the race.
f/s	11	self soft fish sift safe fist shelf
	12	Sef fried six fish for his friends.
g/t	13	got get tog tag toga gate gift goat
	14	Greta got the green toga as a gift.

Review B, Part 1

Review all reaches learned

1. Set the line spacing on your machine to single-space the lines. (Ask your teacher to help you if you do not know how).
2. Key line 1 twice single-spaced (SS); then return twice to double-space (DS) and key line 2 twice SS; then DS and key line 3 twice SS.

Review B, Part 2

Improve technique

Key each line once SS; then DS and key each line again.

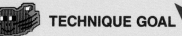 **TECHNIQUE GOAL**

- Snap the tip of the finger toward the palm as you complete each stroke.

 TECHNIQUE GOAL ▶

- Keep your eyes on the copy; keep up your pace to the end of the line.

REVIEW B

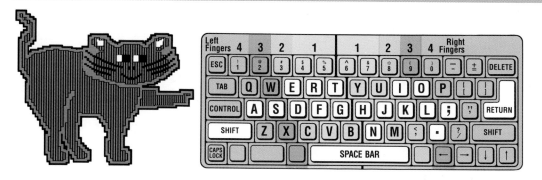

Reach review

```
1  nj gf ol ed .l rf hj tf ik el re at     Return
2  an to if so he it do el go of ha or
3  to dig it; he or she; she is to ski
```

Third-row emphasis

```
1  he she or for go got do dot rid fir     Return
2  is his it tie of off so sod rig dig
3  to too is sir he she re her oak oar
```

Return/enter emphasis

```
4  Jan is gone.              Return without a pause;
5  Hal goes at nine.         start new line quickly.
6  Jae is to go at three.
7  Ned is to take their files.
8  I shall take the train at eight.
```

Apply your skill

1. Side margins: 40-space line.
2. Line spacing: DS.
3. Tab stop: 5 spaces.
4. Key the story line for line.

5. Think about the coins you use at the store.
6. As you key each sentence, insert (key) the number that correctly completes each sentence.

COUNTING PENNIES

Ginny asked her mom for some money to buy a candy bar. Her mother gave her a dollar to buy two candy bars. Ginny could eat one and bring the other one home to her brother, Nick.

Ginny walked to the store and bought a roll of lifesavers for herself. She bought a peppermint patty for Nick. Nick liked peppermint. The clerk at the store gave Ginny the candy and the change left from the dollar. The change she received was in pennies.

When Ginny got home, she gave the peppermint candy to Nick. She gave her mother the pennies. Ginny counted 25 pennies. She wondered how many pennies she had spent.

Think as you key

1 One nickel equals _____ pennies.

2 One dime equals _____ nickels.

3 Five nickels equal _____ quarter.

4 Four quarters equal _____ dollar.

5 Three quarters equal _____ pennies.

6 Ginny had _____ pennies left over.

Improve speed

Key each line twice SS; DS below each 2-line group.

TECHNIQUE GOAL ▶

- Think each word; key it as a unit. Space right after a word and begin the next one.

TECHNIQUE GOAL ▶

- Keep keying until you finish a word; don't stop or slow down between letters.

TECHNIQUE GOAL ▶

- Keep moving steadily from word to word. Try to complete each sentence without stopping.

Short words

1 if it is to do so or go of an ah ha   Return

2 dog for all rid jak sit the off and

3 of an|to go|do so|it is|if he|ah so

Longer words

4 land girl dish lake heel then eight

5 odor fish halt jell hand door fight

6 to land|or risk|is then|of the lake

Easy sentences

7 Jane is to go to the lake for fish.

8 Kal is to aid the girl on the skis.

9 Len is to rig a sail for the skiff.

Lesson 28, Part C

Improve keyboarding technique

Key each pair of lines twice SS (slowly, then faster); DS below each 4-line group.

 **GOALS** ▶

- down-and-in spacing
- out-and-down shifting

Space bar

1 pan jay men pay jam pen lay hen ivy
2 by it|is an|it may|the man|for them
3 He is to tie it to the big oak pen.
4 I am to pay for the key to the bus.

Shift keys and LOCK

5 Aisha and Kyle are back from Dover.
6 Max sent Crystal a ring from Spain.
7 Zoe must read A TALE OF TWO CITIES.
8 Stacy and I will go to USPS Friday.

Lesson 28, Part D

Improve keyboarding response patterns

1. Key each line twice SS (slowly, then faster); DS below each 2-line group.
2. Take two 1′ writings on line 9; find *GWAM* on each.

 **GOALS** ▶

- lines 1–3 slowly, letter by letter
- lines 4–6 quickly, word by word
- lines 7–9, change speed to fit difficulty of word

Letter response

1 draw jump text join fact pink acres
2 pink tag|milk tax|only car|upon you
3 Jim was in a jump seat as you read.

Word response

4 pair auto maps wish half name goals
5 sign the|such men|soap box|auto key
6 Sign the form and own the big auto.

Combination response

7 aid him did act she was own gas bid
8 is set|to him|an act|he ate|it gave
9 She gave the car to him for a test.

1′ GWAM | 1 | 2 | 3 | 4 | 5 | 6 | 7 |

Learn new keys: U and C

1. Learn the location of new keys **u** and **c** by following the standard plan (see page 19).
2. Key each set of 3 lines twice SS: once slowly, again at a faster speed.

Reach technique for u

Reach *up* with *right first* finger.

Reach technique for c

Reach *down* with *left second* finger.

LESSON 7

Learn U

1 j u uj uj us us due due fur fur sue   Return

2 u uj uj ju ju us us jug jug due due

3 to us; is due; for us; the rug; sue

Learn C

4 d c cd cd dc dc cod cod cot cot tic

5 c cd cd cod cod cog cog tic tic cot

6 a tic; a cod; has a cog; at the cot

Combine U and C

7 c u cue cue cut cut cur cur cud cud

8 a cut; the cue; her cud; at the cue

9 is a cur; of the clue; cut the cake

Lesson 28, Part A

Keyboard review and mastery

Key each line twice SS: once slowly, again at a faster speed. DS below each 2-line group.

LESSON 28

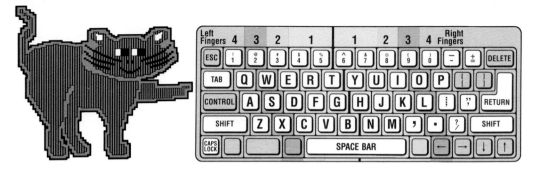

Keyboard review (all letters/figures used)

1 quo 179 win 286 put 075 key 834 mix

2 19 boats|30 ropes|74 buoys|85 flags

3 Jack has a dog; Zahn has five cats.

Lesson 28, Part B

Letter emphasis drill

Each line contains at least 5 uses of the letter shown in color at its left.

1. Key each line once DS.
2. Key again any line(s) that caused you trouble.

Letter emphasis drill

s Sid is sure to see the show at six.

t Tina is to talk to the new student.

u Uri is sure our urn has much value.

v Val has a vivid view of the valley.

w Walt will show us how to use a wok.

x Xie coaxed six oxen by a flax cart.

y Yes, you may take my kayak at four.

z Zelda ate pizza with zeal and zest.

Lesson 7, Part B

Improve keystroking speed

1. Key each set of 3 lines twice SS: once slowly, once more at a faster speed.
2. If time permits, key each set of lines again.

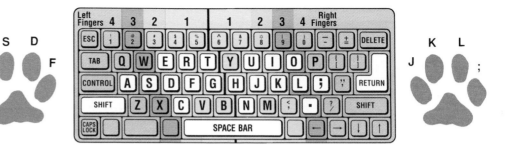

 TECHNIQUE GOAL ▶

- Curl the middle (left second) finger under to strike **c**. Try not to move elbow out.

 TECHNIQUE GOAL ▶

- *Reach* down to strike **shift key** and **. (period)** without moving hand down.

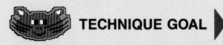 **TECHNIQUE GOAL** ▶

- Speed up between letters within words; space quickly between words.

Practice words and phrases

1 us cud cur cod cog rug fur jug code   Return

2 rush such clue luck just lock ducks

3 on cue; jut out; clue to; good luck

Practice sentences

4 O. J. can use a fur rug in his den.

5 Lt. Han is due at the dock at four.

6 Jud can sell us a duck at the lake.

Practice key words

7 cut urn cod due off the did kit she

8 cue aid fit jut all ask led jet hug

9 cure just lack cuff this gulf thick

Apply your skill

1. Side margins: 40-space line.
2. Line spacing: DS.
3. Tab stop: 5 spaces.
4. Key the story line for line.

5. Read each think-as-you-key statement at the right.
6. As you key each sentence, insert (key) a word or term from the line at the bottom of the page to complete each sentence.

CLOUDS

Lions and sheep and monkeys moving overhead. Big fluffy clouds in animal shapes drifting across the blue sky. I make a list of the animals I see in the clouds. I add to it every day. I list the date, time, and animal shape I see.

My teacher looks at my list. She is happy that I was so careful as I made it. One day I saw a dinosaur. Another day I saw a tree toad. Once my mother and I saw three huge elephants dancing across the heavens.

I wanted to read about clouds, for I knew clouds could not be animals. I asked my brother to go to the library with me so I could read about clouds. We found out that clouds are made of water drops so tiny they float on air. I was happy to know more about clouds.

Think as you key

1 Round white clouds look like _____ .
2 On an ice cream cloud I would put a _____ .
3 A white cloud could be _____ ice cream.
4 A gray cloud brings _____ .
5 _____ lights up a cloud with a big flash.

ice cream | cherry | vanilla | rain | Lightning

**Learn new keys:
W and right shift key**

1. Learn the location of new keys **w** and **right shift** by following the standard plan.
2. Key each set of 3 lines twice SS: once slowly, again at a faster speed.

Reach technique for w

Reach *up* with *left third* finger.

Control of right shift key

Reach *down* with *right little* finger; shift, strike, release.

LESSON 8

Learn W

1   S W WS WS OW OW SOW SOW WOW WOW COW

2   W WS WS SW SW OW OW COW COW OWN OWN

3   so low; we sow; to own; to show how

Learn **right shift key**

4   A; A; Al Al; Sol or Di; Flo and Rod

5   Aida lost to Rog; Don lost to Elsa.

6   Flo is in Duluth; she is to see Al.

Combine W and **right shift key**

7   Willa went to Rio; Walt got a note.

8   Gower said he will see Wes in town.

9   Wendi will go to Waco in two weeks.

Lesson 27, Part C

Review spacing with punctuation

Key each line twice SS; DS below each 2-line group.

RECALL ▼

- Space twice after end-of-sentence punctuation marks (. and ?).
- Space once after within-sentence marks ; and , but twice after :
- Space once after . at end of initial or abbreviation.

Lesson 27, Part D

Build keyboarding speed

1. Take two 15″ writings on each line. If you finish a line before time is called, start over. *GWAM* is shown word for word.

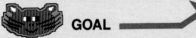 **GOAL**

- To finish keying the line just as time is called.

2. Take two 1′ writings on the ¶. See how many words you can key in a minute.

To find *GWAM:* Read the nearest number (or dot) above the point at which you stopped.

Spacing with punctuation marks

1 Brian is my name; I am called B. J.
2 Mr. Oaks, my teacher, is a big man.
3 Grocery list: ham, eggs, and milk.
4 Is Joan here? It is time to begin.
5 I use No. for North, So. for South.

Sentence timed writing

15″ GWAM

| | 4| | 8| | 12| | 16| | 20| | 24| | 28| |

1 He is the envy of all the lake men.
2 She is to lend a hand to the girls.
3 He may vie for the right to own it.
4 She laid the keys on the oak shelf.

Paragraph timed writing

| All letters used | Easy | 1.2 si | 5.1 awl | 90% hfw |

```
            .        2        .        4        .        6
        Just take it easy; do not try
      .   8       .      10       .      12      .
too hard.  You will not build high
    14       .     16       .     18       .     20
speed if you are lazy, but you can
      .      22       .     24       .     26      .
try too hard.  To excel, keep your
    28       .     30       .     32       .     34
hands quiet; move just the fingers.
```

Improve keystroking speed

1. Key each set of 3 lines twice SS: once slowly, once more at a faster speed.
2. If time permits, key each set of lines again.

Keep fingers curved

Keep fingers upright

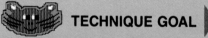 **TECHNIQUE GOAL** ▶

- Speed up between letters within words; space quickly between words.

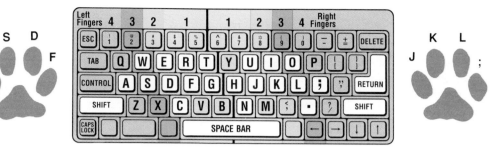

Practice words and phrases

1 an ow go we and own end cow jak row

2 work with worn wood town gown shown

3 an owl; to own; in a wok; he won it

Practice sentences

4 We shall get a new car all our own.

5 Will went to work at the town dock.

6 Gina can win the race if she tries.

Practice key words

7 go an or to is do if as in so we it

8 and she own cut oak urn jog off all

9 rush worn hand corn sick turn right

Keyboard review and mastery

Key each line twice SS: once slowly, again at a faster speed. DS below each 2-line group.

LESSON 27

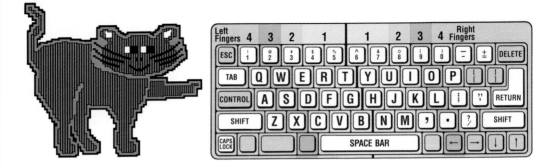

Keyboard review (all letters used)

1 quiz keep axle such corn have major

2 to do of it may go is with but they

3 Vida quit her job at the new plaza.

Lesson 27, Part B

Letter emphasis drill

Each line contains at least 5 uses of the letter shown in color at its left.

1. Key each line once DS.
2. Key again any line(s) that caused you trouble.

Letter emphasis drill

j Jen just jumped with joy at a joke.
k Kurt kept a key in a jacket pocket.
l Luella will let all the girls play.
m Mel met me at the gym for the meet.
n Nina is next; she can win a bronze.
o Otis is old enough to go to school.
p Pima, please pick up a party prize.
q Quade is quite quick so Quent quit.
r Ria ran into the surf after a crab.

Learn new keys: B and Y

1. Learn the location of new keys **b** and **y** by following the standard plan.
2. Key each set of 3 lines twice SS: once slowly, again at a faster speed.

Reach technique for b

Reach *down* with *left first* finger.

Reach technique for y

Reach *up* with *right first* finger.

LESSON 9

Learn b

1   f b b bf bf fib fib rob rob but but

2   b bf bf rub rub bid bid but but job

3   to fib; or rob; and rub; a big job;

Learn y

4   j y y yj yj jay jay lay lay hay hay

5   y yj yj jay jay eye eye say say day

6   a jay; an eye; is to say; for a day

Combine b and y

7   bf yj by by buy buy boy boy bye bye

8   by it; to be; go by; to buy; by you

9   buy it; lay by; by and by; but your

Apply your skill

1. Side margins: 35-space line.
2. Line spacing: DS.
3. Tab stop: 5 spaces.
4. Key the story line for line.

5. Read each think-as-you-key state-ment at the right.
6. As you key each sentence, insert (key) in the blank the word or words from the story that cor-rectly completes each sentence.

EXPLORER DANNY

Danny liked to play in the woods behind his house and pretend that it was a forest. He liked to climb the trees and look down at the ground. As he watched his dog walk under the trees, he pretended it was a bear.

Danny liked to think that he was an explorer. Even his name was the name of an explorer, Daniel Boone. Danny wished his backyard was a wild, new land that no one else had ever seen.

In this new land, Danny would catch his own food. He would take a bath in the stream. He would live in a log cabin and cook over an open fire. He would pick a tree he could cut down to build his log cabin.

Think as you key

1 _____ is the main character or person.
2 Danny pretended he was an _____ .
3 He imagined his dog to be a _____ .
4 He pretended he lived in a _____ .
5 Danny would make his cabin from a _____ .

Improve keystroking technique

1. Key each set of 3 lines twice SS: once slowly, once more at a faster speed.
2. If time permits, key each set of lines again.

 TECHNIQUE GOAL ▶

- Make up and down reaches with the fingers without moving the hand up or down and without moving the elbow in or out.

 TECHNIQUE GOAL ▶

- Use a 1-2-3 count in shifting: (1) shift, (2) strike key to be capped, and (3) release both keys.

 TECHNIQUE GOAL ▶

- Speed up between letters within words; space quickly between words.

Practice words and phrases

1 but yes bye yet buy yen bid boy fob

2 rye sob sly bud cry rib sky bob any

3 to bid; the boy; not yet; blue sky;

Practice sentences (all letters learned)

4 Judy had a yen to buy the baby cub.

5 Dr. Foy knew the boy had blue eyes.

6 G. W. let the baby cry in her crib.

Practice key words

7 by of an to is do if ah or it so go

8 oak got fur she but and own cut jay

9 than work such girl clan idle world

Lesson 26, Part C

Improve keyboarding technique

Key each line twice SS.

 PRACTICE HINT ▶

- *Think, say,* and *key* the words at a brisk pace; space quickly.

 **PRACTICE HINT** ▶

- Shift, strike the key, and release both in a 1-2-3 count.

 **PRACTICE HINT** ▶

- Keep up your pace to the end of the line, return quickly, and start the next line without a pause.

Lesson 26, Part D

Build keyboarding speed

1. Take a 20″ writing on each line. If you finish a line before time is called, start over. *GWAM* is shown word by word.
2. Key the lines again.

 **GOAL** ▶

- To finish keying the line just as time is called.

Space bar (Use down-and-in motion)

1 den pay ban may pan toy men boy ham
2 of ham|to pay|or ban|may be|the pan
3 Rudy is to pay the man for the ham.

Shift keys (Shift; strike key; release both)

4 Ryan Zia is in Maine with Al Payne.
5 Nan and Cora are to see Pam or Zoe.
6 Lee Spahn will meet us in St. Paul.

Return (Finish the line; return; start new line quickly)

7 The goal you set is high.
8 I shall set a high goal, also.
9 Do you think we can make our goals?

20″ GWAM

| | 3 | 6 | 9 | 12 | 15 | 18 | 21 |

1 I may go to the city for the chair.

2 She is to make a map for the girls.

3 When did they visit the lake towns?

4 He and a buddy are to wax the auto.

5 They are to see if the car is tidy.

6 As she saw, the sign was torn down.

Review what you have learned

Key each line twice SS: once slowly, again at a faster speed. DS below each 2-line group.

 TECHNIQUE GOAL ▶

- Make up and down reaches with the fingers without moving the hand up or down and without moving the elbow in or out.

 TECHNIQUE GOAL ▶

- Reduce time between letters and between words; space quickly.

 **GOAL** ▶

- Review spacing after periods used with abbreviations and initials.

REVIEW C

Review reaches learned

1 ed hj ws uj tf nj rf ik cd ol bf yj

2 Guido will buy a house for his dog.

3 Jaye and Jack are now at Bay Shore.

Practice short words and phrases

4 an by us he go do of or if it is to

5 at in as on ad he ad on cab kin was

6 by an|it is|of us|to do|an el|go by

Practice abbreviations and initials

7 Lydia said to send the chair c.o.d.

8 Dr. Hahn said to use rt. for route.

9 J. B. is to go to St. Cloud School.

**Keyboard review
and mastery**

Key each line twice SS: once slowly, again at a faster speed. DS below each 2-line group.

Letter emphasis drill

Each line contains at least 5 uses of the letter shown in color at its left.

1. Key each line once DS.
2. Key again any line(s) that caused you trouble.

LESSON 26

Reach review (all letters used)

```
1   za ?; xs .l cd ,k vf mj bf nj qa p;

2   ws ol ed ik rf uj tf yj gf hj a; fj

3   aqua just kick fled slow rode swing
```

Letter emphasis drill

```
a  Aida has a plan that all can apply.
b  Bob can buy a book at my book barn.
c  Cyd can cash a check at the office.
d  Don fled down the road toward town.
e  Ella ended her report with a quote.
f  Flo fell off a boat but feels fine.
g  Greg got a gold medal not long ago.
h  Helen held her hands over her head.
i  Ian is to swim in the big inn pool.
```

Review C, Part 2

Improve keystroking speed

1. Key each set of 3 lines twice SS: once slowly, once more at a faster speed.
2. If time permits, key each set of lines again.

Fingers curved

Fingers upright

Strike down

Snap toward you

Practice longer words and phrases

1 both duty hang rich with rush chair

2 just risk lend fish turn flak their

3 to buy it; is a risk; work with us;

Practice sentences (all letters learned)

4 You are to be at the field by four.

5 Byron is to go by the lake to fish.

6 Jane can do the sign work for cash.

Review C, Part 3

Combine sentences into a paragraph

Key the paragraph twice; double-space (DS) between lines each time. At the end of a line, do not stop; return quickly and begin the next line.

Practice a paragraph (all letters learned)

A few days ago I got a dog. He is

just nine weeks old. He has curly

black hair and white ears and feet.

UNIT 4

YOU BUILD AND APPLY KEYBOARDING SKILL

Lessons 26-34

YOUR GOALS

In this unit of 8 lessons, you will:

1. Review the alphabetic keyboard
2. Review the number-row keys
3. Improve keyboarding technique and speed
4. Learn to apply your skill
5. Measure what you have learned

Learn new keys: M and X

1. Learn the location of new keys **m** and **x** by following the standard plan.
2. Key each set of 3 lines twice SS: once slowly, again at a faster speed.

Reach technique for m

Reach *down* with *right first* finger.

Reach technique for x

Reach *down* with *left third* finger.

LESSON 10

Learn m

1　j m mj mj me me am am ma ma jam jam

2　m mj mj jam jam ham ham may may man

3　am to; or me; if ma; is ham; of jam

Learn X

4　s x x xs xs ox ox ax ax six six fix

5　x xs xs six six fix fix fox fox box

6　an ox; an ax; a box; to fix; by six

Combine m and X

7　m x am ox me ax ham six jam fox men

8　a ham; an ox; a box; a mix; for six

9　am to fix; jam for six; box the ham

Practice commonly used symbol keys

1. Key each line twice SS; DS below each 2-line group.
2. As time permits, rekey selected lines until you can reach each key without looking.

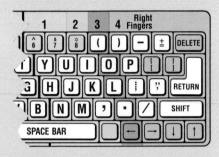

Lesson 25, Part C

Key paragraphs containing figures/symbols

1. Take two 1' writings on ¶ 1; find *GWAM*.
2. Take two 1' writings on ¶ 2; find *GWAM*.
3. Compare *GWAM* scores.
4. Take another 1' writing on the slower ¶ to build speed.

To find *GWAM:* Read the nearest number (or dot) above the point at which you stopped.

1 Daryl asked, "Can't we be friends?"
2 I got a 1-way ticket; she, a 2-way.
3 Shift for +, but don't shift for =.
4 Coila said, "It's your turn to go."
5 She said, "Key 3/5 (three fifths)."
6 I use first- and fourth-class mail.
7 Melba (our captain) won the debate.
8 See pages 8–26 for fractions (1/3).
9 Marvin, it's a 14- by 18-foot room.
10 Use the = and + signs in equations.
11 I studied Unit 3 (pp. 26–37) today.
12 "That's my aunt," she said proudly.

All letters and figures used

     .   2   .   4   .   6
    Skill at a keyboard is a major
  .   8   .   10   .   12   .
one you can prize for life. It may
  14   .   16   .   18   .   20
give you quite an edge in your work
  .   22   .   24   .   26   .
at school and, next, in a good job.
         .   2   .   4   .   6
    Learn to key by touch the fig-
  .   8   .   10   .   12   .
ures 1 through 0. Figures, such as
  14   .   16   .   18   .   20
28 and 49, are fairly easy; others,
  .   22   .   24   .   26   .
such as 135 and 670, harder to key.

Lesson 10, Part B

Improve keystroking technique

1. Key each set of 3 lines twice SS: once slowly, once more at a faster speed.
2. If time permits, key each set of lines again.

 TECHNIQUE GOAL ▶

- Keep the hands steady; avoid moving them forward (away from you) or downward (toward you).

TECHNIQUE GOAL ▶

- Keep the elbows still; avoid moving them in or out as you key the copy.

Lesson 10, Part C

Combine sentences into a paragraph

Key the paragraph twice DS. At the end of a line, do not stop; return quickly and begin the next line.

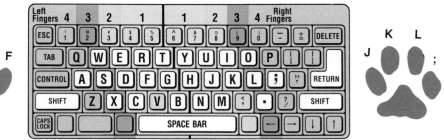

Practice words and phrases

1 ox am ax me six man fox may fix jam

2 make flex name flax form oxen small

3 of six|am to fix|am too lax|may mix

Practice sentences

4 She may fix the box as I mark flax.

5 Jake can mix a glass of lime drink.

6 May saw six oxen at a dam in Macao.

Practice a paragraph (all letters learned)

A major goal of mine is to be able soon to key all the letters. With luck I can also excel at good form.

Learn commonly used symbol keys

Use the table at the right to learn the name, location, and technique for keying commonly used symbols on Apple, IBM, and Tandy computers.

1. Locate the apostrophe key using the table; then find it on your keyboard.
2. Key the matching lines below the table twice each.
3. Locate and practice in the same way each of the other symbols listed in the table.

Additional practice is provided on page 79.

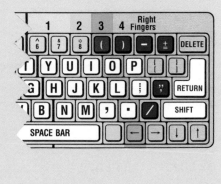

LESSON 25

COMMONLY USED SYMBOLS
APPLE, IBM, AND TANDY

	Name	Symbol	Row/Side	Finger/Direction
	Apostrophe	'	2/right	rt. 4th/right
	Diagonal	/	1/right	rt. 4th/down
	Equals	=	4/right	rt. 4th/up
	Hyphen	–	4/right	rt. 4th/up
Shifted	Parenthesis, left	(	4/right	rt. 3d/up
	Parenthesis, right	)	4/right	rt. 4th/up
	Plus	+	4/right	rt. 4th/up
	Quote marks	"	2/right	rt. 4th/right

' 1 ; ' ; ' '; '; it's; I'll; It's his.
  2 Joi, dot the i's and cross the t's.

/ 3 ; / ; / /; /; 2/3 Key 5/6 and 3/10.
  4 Ed, does 2/3 plus 3/4 equal 1 5/12?

= 5 ; = ; = =; =; Does 17 plus 28 = 45?
  6 Did she say that 12 times 12 = 144?

- 7 ; - ; - -; -; 4-foot; 25-cent stamp
  8 We have both 4-ply and 6-ply tires.

() 9 9 (0) (9)0 (90); I shift for ().
  10 Key: (1) I'd; (2) We'll; (3) He'd.

+ 11 ; + ; + +; +; 1 + 4 + 10 + 20 = 35.
  12 Does 15 + 17 = 32 and 16 + 19 = 35?

" 13 ; " ; " "; "; ;"; "I can," he said.
  14 She asked, "Don't you want to eat?"

Learn new keys: P and V

1. Learn the location of new keys **p** and **v** by following the standard plan.
2. Key each set of 3 lines twice SS: once slowly, again at a faster speed.

Reach technique for p

Reach *up* with *right little* finger.

Reach technique for v

Reach *down* with *left first* finger.

LESSON 11

Learn **p**

1   ; p p p; p; pa pa up up lap lap pen

2   p; p; pa pa; up up apt apt pen pens

3   a pen; a cup; is up; an ape; pay up

Learn **V**

4   f v v vf vf via via vie vie vim vim

5   v vf vf van van have have five five

6   go via; vie for; has vim; has a van

Combine **p** and **V**

7   p v up vie cup van cap vim rap five

8   go up; a van; a cup; to vie; apt to

9   to dive; pave it; give up; very apt

Lesson 24, Part B

Improve technique on copy containing numbers

Key each line twice SS (slowly, then faster); DS below each 2-line group.

 **GOALS** ▶

- curved, upright fingers
- wrists low, relaxed
- hands as quiet (motionless) as possible

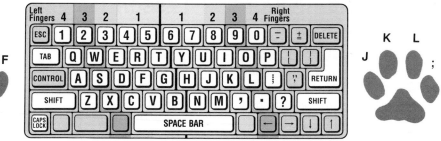

1 0; 5f 9l 3d 7j 2s 8k 4f 6j 1a 46203

2 by 56 so 29 he 63 cup 370 vial 4819

3 Key numbers 497, 362, 405, and 168.

4 My ZIP Code is 48261; his is 37509.

Lesson 24, Part C

Improve keyboarding speed

1. Key each line twice SS (slowly, then faster); DS below each 2-line group.
2. As time permits, take three 1' writings on line 7; find *GWAM* on each writing.

Use the scale under line 7 to find *GWAM.*

All letters used

1 Luan got a prize for her six poems.

2 Cy won the match on the last serve.

3 The sky turned grey then jet black.

4 Did she quiz you on the field trip?

5 Pam wore a blue tutu in the ballet.

6 I can key each word at a fair pace.

7 Bo is to go with me to the ski tow.

1' GWAM | 1 | 2 | 3 | 4 | 5 | 6 | 7 |

Lesson 11, Part B

Improve keystroking technique

1. Key each set of 3 lines twice SS: once slowly, once more at a faster speed.
2. If time permits, key each set of lines again.

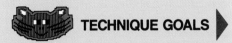 **TECHNIQUE GOALS** ▶

- Reach up to the **p** and down to **v** with the fingers; keep your hands steady.
- Avoid twisting your hand out at the wrist as you reach to the **p**.

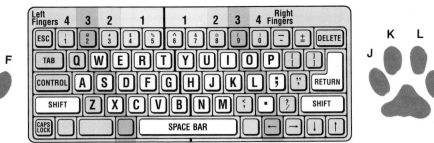

Practice words and phrases

1 nap vim cup fox wig but rug due fog

2 just kept next type land they given

3 has vim; big pan; her van; his play

Practice sentences

4 Bibi has yet to say she will do it.

5 Van may ask to vie for the top job.

6 Ana could make her next goal today.

Lesson 11, Part C

Combine sentences into a paragraph

Key the paragraph twice DS. At the end of a line, do not stop; return quickly and begin the next line.

Practice a paragraph (all letters learned)

My next goal is to do just as well as I can. Good work pays off. By having a goal I get more work done.

Learn new keys: 2 and 6

1. Learn the location of new keys **2** and **6** by following the standard plan.
2. Key each set of 3 lines twice SS: once slowly, again at a faster speed.

LESSON 24

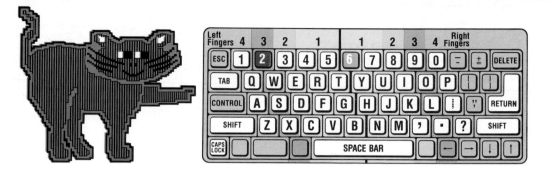

Reach technique for 2

Reach *up* with *left third* finger.

Reach technique for 6

Reach *up* with *right first* finger.

Learn 2

1 s 2 s 2 2s 2s s2s s2s Key number 2.

2 Try 2 and 22. Study pages 2 to 22.

3 All 22 have the right answer, 1492.

Learn 6

4 j 6 j 6 6j 6j j6j j6j Key number 6.

5 Try 6 and 66. Did he say 6 or 666?

6 We 6 traveled 66 miles on Route 66.

Combine 2 and 6

7 All 62 pupils took the May 26 quiz.

8 The carton is 22 by 16 by 6 inches.

9 Key 17, 26, 38, 40, and 59, please.

Learn new keys:
Q and , (comma)

1. Learn the location of new keys **q** and **,** (comma) by following the standard plan.

2. Key each set of 3 lines twice SS: once slowly, again at a faster speed.

Reach technique for q

Reach *up* with *left little* finger.

Reach technique for , (comma)

Reach *down* with *right second* finger; space once after **,** used as punctuation.

LESSON 12

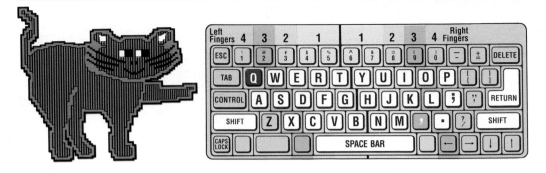

Learn **q**

1 a qa qa aq aq quo quo qt. qt. quick

2 qa qa quit quit aqua aqua quip quip

3 a qt.; a quay; a quip; he has squid

Learn **,** (comma)

4 k ,k ,k k,k k,k Ask Vi, Max, or Al.

5 Peg, go with me; Di, stay with Max.

6 Pick to, too, or two and key it in.

Combine **q** and **,**

7 Key the words quit, aqua, and quay.

8 Quen quit my squad; Quig quit, too.

9 Velma, use sq. ft. for square feet.

Lesson 23, Part B

Improve technique on copy containing numbers

Key each line twice SS (slowly, then faster); DS below each 2-line group.

 **GOALS** ▶

- keep the hands as quiet (motionless) as possible
- reach the *fingers* to the top row; do not move the whole hand up.

1 la 7j 3d 9l 4f 8k 5f 0; do 39 or 94

2 Mela sold 85 tickets; Toby sold 90.

3 The 473 pencils cost 10 cents each.

Lesson 23, Part C

Improve keyboarding speed

1. Key the ¶ once SS at an easy, steady pace; do not pause between the letters and words.
2. As time permits, key the ¶ again. Try a faster speed.

I have a cat named Hera and a dog named Zeus. They are very good friends. Once in a while, though, when Hera sneaks up against Zeus and wants to play, he gets mad and snaps at her. She hisses back, and Zeus jumps up and chases Hera up a tree. He keeps her up there a long time. Like people, dogs and cats do not like each other sometimes.

Lesson 12, Part B

Improve keystroking technique

1. Key each set of 3 lines twice SS: once slowly, once more at a faster speed.
2. If time permits, key each set of lines again.

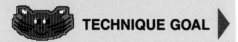 **TECHNIQUE GOAL** ▶

- Reach up to **q** without moving the elbow out.

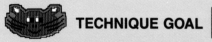 **TECHNIQUE GOAL** ▶

- Curl the right second finger down to **, (comma)** without moving the hand toward you.

Lesson 12, Part C

Combine sentences into a paragraph

Key the paragraph twice DS. At the end of a line, do not stop; return quickly and begin the next line.

Practice phrases (word groups)

1 sq. yds. |she quit |is aqua |the squad

2 he quit |aqua blue |is quiet |to quote

3 an aqua sea |is a quail |a quick quip

Practice sentences

4 Her squad is quick, but so is mine.

5 When he said squid, he meant squib.

6 If Max quits, your squad will lose.

Practice a paragraph (all letters learned)

Do not quit now; keep on. You are doing fine. You can make the next goal; just give it a bit more time.

Learn new keys: 3 and 0

1. Learn the location of new keys **3** and **0 (zero)** by following the standard plan.
2. Key each set of 3 lines twice SS: once slowly, again at a faster speed.

Reach technique for 3

Reach *up* with *left second* finger.

Reach technique for 0

Reach *up* with *right little* finger.

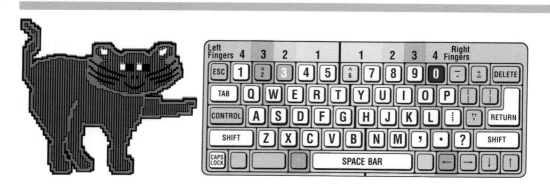

Learn **3**

1 d 3 d 3 3d 3d d3d d3d Key number 3.

2 Try 3 and 33. Just 3 of 33 are in.

3 We keyed for 3 minutes at 33 w.a.m.

Learn **0**

4 ; 0 ; 0 0; 0; ;0; ;0; Key 0 and 00.

5 Try grade 00; it is finer than a 0.

6 Please get 50 pads and 100 pencils.

Combine **3** and **0**

7 Did only 3 of the 30 pupils key 30?

8 We sold 300 hot dogs and 503 colas.

9 Do Items 3, 5, 7, and 10, page 489.

Reach review

Key each line twice SS: once slowly, again at a faster speed. DS below each 2-line group.

REVIEW D

 TECHNIQUE GOALS ▶

- Make each reach by "touch" (without looking at your keyboard).
- Reach down to shift key without moving hands.

 **TECHNIQUE GOALS** ▶

- Think each word; try to key it as a unit.
- Keep fingers curved and upright.

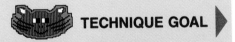 **TECHNIQUE GOAL** ▶

- Key each phrase without pausing or stopping between words. Keep moving to the next word.

Reach review (all reaches learned)

1 hj gf yj tf uj rf ik ed ol ws p; qa

2 mj vf nj bf ,k cd .l xs ju fr lo sw

3 Jae Coe|Rod Marx|Nan Epps|Pat Spahn

Practice key words (all letters learned)

4 via may six pan for own and the lay

5 cut she box jam fog oak row but quo

6 they firm such girl just quit spend

Practice phrases (all letters learned)

7 of us|to me|by it|if he|do it|is an

8 the van|and got|for pay|all six own

9 her job is|she kept it|she can quit

Lesson 22, Part B

Improve technique on copy containing numbers

Key each line twice SS (slowly, then faster); DS below each 2-line group.

 **GOALS**

- quiet hands and arms
- steady pace (no pauses)

NOTE: When a : is used in expressing time, do not space after it. (see line 4)

Lesson 22, Part C

Improve keyboarding speed

1. Take a 15″ timed writing on each line. If you finish a line before time is called, start over. Find *GWAM*.
2. Key the lines again.

 **GOAL**

- To finish keying the line just as time is called.

1 Review pages 47 to 59 and 81 to 89.

2 Key 17, 48, 59, 88, 44, 77, and 99.

3 I checked lockers 84, 117, and 195.

4 All 7 arrived at 8:45 on August 19.

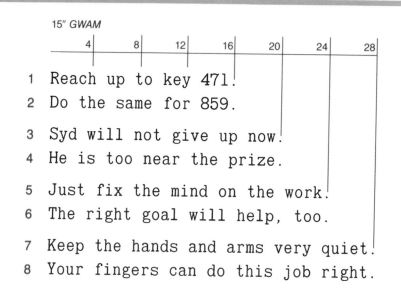

15″ GWAM

| | 4 | | 8 | | 12 | | 16 | | 20 | | 24 | | 28 |

1 Reach up to key 471.
2 Do the same for 859.

3 Syd will not give up now.
4 He is too near the prize.

5 Just fix the mind on the work.
6 The right goal will help, too.

7 Keep the hands and arms very quiet.
8 Your fingers can do this job right.

Review D, Part 2

Improve keystroking speed on sentences

1. Take a 20-second (20″) timed writing on each sentence. Your rate in gross words a minute (*GWAM*) is shown word for word above the lines.
2. Take another 20″ writing on each line. Try to increase speed.

NOTE: If you finish a line before 20″ are up, start over.

Review D, Part 3

Combine sentences into a paragraph

Key the paragraph twice DS: once slowly to get the feel of the words, then again to speed up keystroking.

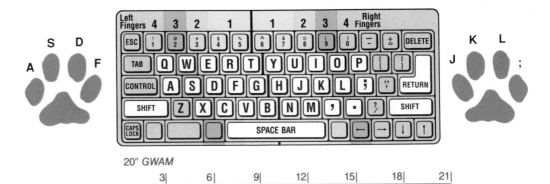

20″ GWAM

| | 3| | 6| | 9| | 12| | 15| | 18| | 21| |

1 Vi is to go to the city for an urn.

2 Ana is to do the map work for them.

3 Dorn is to fix the pen for the man.

4 The girl is to pay the city for it.

5 Rick got the dog at a mall in town.

6 Quen is in the city to see his mom.

7 Jane ate at an inn by the big lake.

8 I shall get a form for you by noon.

Practice a paragraph (all letters learned)

I like to feed the many birds that live in our yard. I see six quail and two jays pecking for seeds now.

Learn new keys: 5 and 9

1. Learn the location of new keys **5** and **9** by following the standard plan.
2. Key each set of 3 lines twice SS: once slowly, again at a faster speed.

Reach technique for 5

Reach *up* with *left first* finger.

Reach technique for 9

Reach *up* with *right third* finger.

LESSON 22

Learn 5

1 f 5 f 5 5f 5f f5f f5f Key figure 5.

2 Add 5 and 55. Of 55, just 5 wrote.

3 Tia weighs 75 pounds; her dad, 155.

Learn 9

Use the letter "l"

4 l 9 l 9 9l 9l l9l l9l Key figure 9.

Use the figure 1

5 Add 9 and 99. Count out 49 of 199.

6 They met from 8 to 9 a.m. on May 9.

Combine 5 and 9

7 As 4 from 9 is 5, 44 from 99 is 55.

8 Check Room 79 first, then go to 85.

9 My club has 194 girls and 185 boys.

Learn new keys:
Z and : (colon)

1. Learn the location of new keys **z** and **:** (colon) by following the standard plan.
2. Key each set of 3 lines twice SS: once slowly, again at a faster speed.

Reach technique for z

Reach *down* with *left little* finger.

Reach technique for : (colon)

Left shift and strike **;** key; space twice after **:** used as punctuation.

LESSON 13

Learn Z

1 a z z za za zap zap zip zip zoo zoo

2 za za oz. oz. zap zap zoo zoo dozen

3 a zit; an oz.; a doz.; lazy zoo day

Learn : (colon)

4 ; : : :; :; Dear Di: Shift for a :

5 :; :; Date: Time: Name: Dear Al:

6 Dear Mr. Ho: Take these six steps:

Combine Z and :

7 Key these words: zap, lazy, dozen.

8 Call these pupils: Roz, Zane, Zoe.

9 My address: One West Zania Circle.

Lesson 21, Part B

Improve technique on copy containing numbers

Key each line twice SS (slowly, then faster); DS below each 2-line group.

 **GOAL** ▶

- reach the *fingers* to the top row; do not move the whole hand up.

Lesson 21, Part C

Improve keyboarding speed

1. Take a 15" timed writing on each line. If you finish a line before time is called, start over. Find *GWAM*.
2. Key the lines again.

 **GOAL** ▶

- To finish keying the line just as time is called.

1 Can you key 18, 47, and 48 quickly?

2 Reach up with speed for 17 and 184.

3 Get 74 blue flags and 188 red ones.

4 Bring me 184 forms and 174 pencils.

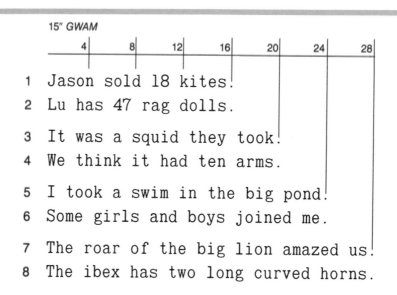

15" GWAM

| | 4 | 8 | 12 | 16 | 20 | 24 | 28 |

1 Jason sold 18 kites!

2 Lu has 47 rag dolls.

3 It was a squid they took!

4 We think it had ten arms.

5 I took a swim in the big pond!

6 Some girls and boys joined me.

7 The roar of the big lion amazed us!

8 The ibex has two long curved horns.

Lesson 13, Part B

Improve keystroking technique

1. Key each line twice SS: once slowly, once more at a faster speed.
2. If time permits, key each line again.

 **TECHNIQUE GOALS** ▶

- Reach with the fingers; keep the hands in place.
- Shift, strike letter to be capped, and release both keys (1-2-3).

Lesson 13, Part C

Combine sentences into a paragraph

Key the paragraph twice DS: once slowly to get the feel of the words, then again to speed up keystroking.

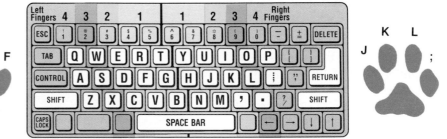

Practice sentences

1 I shall pay the men to do the work.

2 Cody is to work on the sign for us.

3 Aida is to go to the zoo with them.

4 Karla may quit work at five or six.

5 Iris kept the bird in a large cage.

6 Jose then put the pen on the shelf.

7 I am to go with Sue, Max, and Skip.

8 Goal: fingers curved; hands quiet.

Practice a paragraph (all letters used)

To be a whiz at this work can give me joy. The next goal is to build fair speed. I can do this quickly.

Learn new keys: 4 and 8

1. Learn the location of new keys **4** and **8** by following the standard plan.
2. Key each set of 3 lines twice SS: once slowly, again at a faster speed.

Reach technique for 4

Reach *up* with *left first* finger.

Reach technique for 8

Reach *up* with *right second* finger.

LESSON 21

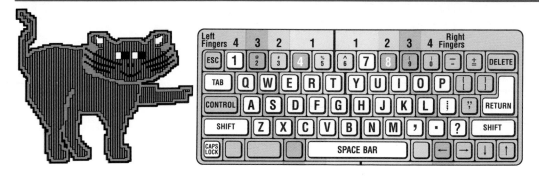

Learn 4

1 f 4 f 4 4f 4f f4f f4f Key figure 4.

2 Add 4 and 44. Only 4 of 44 can go.

3 We meet from 4 to 7 p.m. on May 14.

Learn 8

4 k 8 k 8 8k 8k k8k k8k Key figure 8.

5 Add 8 and 88. Of 88, they chose 8.

6 In 8 days I will be 8. Are you 18?

Combine 4 and 8

7 If 4 from 8 is 4, 44 from 88 is 44.

8 Den 4 played Den 8. Did 7 play 18?

9 Mom said our lot is 74 by 188 feet.

Learn new keys: CAPS LOCK and ? (question mark)

1. Learn the location of new keys **CAPS LOCK** and **? (question mark)** by following the standard plan.
2. Key each set of 3 lines twice SS: once slowly, again at a faster speed.

Reach technique for LOCK

Reach *left* and *down* with *left little* finger.

Reach technique for ? (question)

Left shift; reach *down* with *right little* finger; space twice after **?** at end of sentence.

NOTE: Depress the LOCK and leave it down until the ALL-CAP combination has been typed. Strike the LOCK again to return to regular capital-and-lowercase typing.

LESSON 14

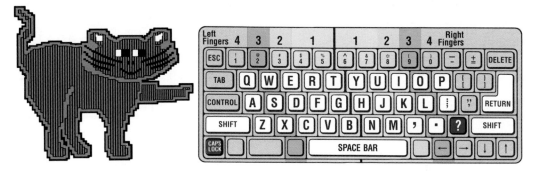

Learn **CAPS LOCK** (Find CAPS LOCK; use left little finger.)

1 NBC and CBS |WLW or WKRC |WGN and USA

2 The USPS asks us to use a ZIP CODE.

3 The UCLA game will be shown by ABC.

Learn **?** (question mark)

4 ; ? ? ?; ?; Who? Who? Who is she?

5 When did she go? Shall we go, too?

6 Do you know why Masami is not here?

Combine **CAPS LOCK** and **?**

7 Did she use the UP ARROW or ESCAPE?

8 Does she use the LOCK for ALL CAPS?

9 Did you read the book OLIVER TWIST?

Lesson 20, Part B

Improve technique on copy containing numbers

Key each line twice SS (slowly, then faster); DS below each 2-line group.

 **GOALS**

- keep unused fingers as close to home keys as you can
- reach as far as you can with the finger to strike a key on the top row

1 We will meet in Room 1 on August 7.

2 I missed 7 on Quiz 7; 1 on Quiz 17.

3 Check No. 1771 is dated January 11.

Lesson 20, Part C

Improve keyboarding speed

As you learn long reaches to the numbers, you are likely to key in jerks and pauses and lose speed. In these number lessons, you will key sentences and paragraphs to help you improve your speed.

1. Key the paragraphs (¶s) once SS; DS between ¶s. Keep up a steady pace; do not pause.
2. As time permits, key the ¶s a second time. Try a faster pace.

A dove coos its sad song in a nearby tree. A cricket begins an endless chirp. A dog howls in the distance. A baby cries its hunger pains.

Lights dot the gray dusk. A gust of wind rustles the leaves of a tree then dies away. A lone star blinks in the purple sky.

Night falls.

Lesson 14, Part B

Improve keystroking technique

1. Key each line twice SS: once slowly, once more at a faster speed.
2. If time permits, key each line again.

Space:

- once after ; and ,
- twice after . and ? at end of sentence
- once after . at end of initials and abbreviations, but do not space after . within small-letter abbreviations

Practice sentences (all reaches learned)

1 Ms. Voss took a quick trip to York.

2 He, she, and I fixed a quick snack.

3 B. J. could send the puzzles c.o.d.

4 I used yd. for yard; qt. for quart.

5 Is he going? If so, may I go, too?

6 THINK, but do more than that: ACT.

Lesson 14, Part C

Combine sentences into a paragraph

Key the paragraph twice DS: once slowly to get the feel of the words, then again to speed up keystroking.

Practice a paragraph (all letters used)

The hut next to the river where we camp is quite cozy. But just as I drift off to sleep, the hooting of an owl sends a chill down my back.

Learn new keys: 1 and 7

1. Learn the location of new keys **1** and **7** by following the standard plan (see page 19).
2. Key each set of 3 lines twice SS: once slowly, again at a faster speed.

Reach technique for 1

Reach *up* with *left little* finger.

Reach technique for 7

Reach *up* with *right first* finger.

LESSON 20

Learn 1

1 a l a l la la ala ala Key figure 1.

2 Add 1 and 11. Study pages 1 to 11.

3 Zia is 11. Her twin sisters are 1.

Learn 7

4 j 7 j 7 7j 7j j7j j7j Key figure 7.

5 Key 7 and 77. Did she say 7 or 77?

6 Just 7 of 77 went; all 7 are there.

Combine 1 and 7

7 She said to key 11, 17, 71, and 77.

8 I had 11 fish, 7 birds, and 1 frog.

9 Try room 17, but it may be Room 71.

Reach review

Key each line twice SS: once slowly, again at a faster speed. DS below each 2-line group.

 TECHNIQUE GOAL ▶

- Hands and arms quiet; reach with the fingers.

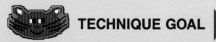 **TECHNIQUE GOAL** ▶

- Key words as units; space quickly between them.

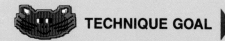 **TECHNIQUE GOAL** ▶

- Key words at a steady pace, letter by letter; keep elbows steady.

LESSON 15

Reach review (all letters used)

```
1  qa p; ws ol ed ik rf uj tf yj gf hj

2  za ?; xs .l cd ,k vf mj bf nj ce un

3  am ox irk zoo fog vie cup job quits
```

Practice easy words (all letters used)

```
4  an if ox so me is am it or go by of

5  cut zoo fix pen map but did got jam

6  both work lake down such quay visit
```

Practice harder words (all letters used)

```
7  we up ad in as on ax my was pop are

8  pin bet you saw ink tax him gas oil

9  cave milk were look faze jump quits
```

UNIT 3

YOU LEARN NUMBER-ROW KEYS

Lessons 20-25

YOUR GOALS

In the 6 lessons of this unit, you will learn:

1. The keyboard location of each number key.
2. The keyboard location of more punctuation keys.
3. How to strike each key properly with the correct finger.
4. How to key sentences and para-graphs containing numbers.

Lesson 15, Part B

Improve keystroking speed on sentences

1. Take a 20-second (20″) timed writing on each sentence. Your rate in gross words a minute (*GWAM*) is shown word for word above the lines.
2. Take another 20″ writing on each line. Try to increase speed.

20″ GWAM

| | 3| | 6| | 9| | 12| | 15| | 18| | 21| |

1 The town is to pay me for the sign.

2 Vic lent me a map of the busy city.

3 Roz paid the man for the lake land.

4 Quen is to fix the city bus for us.

5 Six of the girls fish off the dock.

6 Jen, did you turn right by the zoo?

Lesson 15, Part C

Learn to indent paragraphs

1. Learn how to indent the first line of a paragraph. (Ask your teacher to show you, or use the diskette for Lesson 15.)
2. Key each of the paragraphs shown at the right.
3. If time permits, key them again.

Indented paragraphs (all letters used)

Tab   To be able to key by touch is a skill to prize. I will not quit now, for I want to have good speed.

Tab   My next major goal will be to keep my eyes on the copy. Thus, I can spend all my time keying words.

Lesson 19, Part B

Build keyboarding speed

Key each line twice SS.

 PRACTICE HINT ▶

- *Think, say,* and *key* letter by letter.

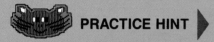 **PRACTICE HINT** ▶

- *Think, say,* and *key* each word as a word.

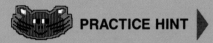 **PRACTICE HINT** ▶

- *Think, say,* and *key* the easy words as *words. Think, say,* and *key* the harder words letter by letter.

Lesson 19, Part C

Measure and build your speed

1. Take a 1-minute (1') writing on the paragraph. See how many words you can key.
2. Read the nearest number (or dot) above the point at which you stopped. That is your 1-minute GWAM.

Practice words by *letter* response

1 you ate ink raw pop age mop tab pin

2 few|you are|pop art|get ink|oil ads

3 Lily saw him eat a crab at my cafe.

Practice words by *word* response

4 bid got man eye pay sir map but fix

5 an auto|to risk|so busy|he paid the

6 Dirk is to pay us for the map work.

Combine *letter* and *word* responses

7 eat air tax bow tie due him for you

8 my duty|as such|on fuel|we both saw

9 It is my duty to bag the best fish.

Paragraph timed writing (all letters used)

```
         .       2     .       4     .       6
    Be quick to size up each word
 .       8     .      10     .      12     .
in the copy, for doing so may help
   14     .      16     .      18     .      20
to add skill.  Next, try to adjust
 .      22     .      24     .      26     .
speed to move smoothly to each key.
```

Improve keystroking speed

Key each line twice SS: once slowly, again at a faster speed. DS below each 2-line group.

 TECHNIQUE GOAL ▶

- Make the space following a word a part of the word.

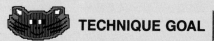 **TECHNIQUE GOAL** ▶

- Keep moving steadily across the line—no pauses.

Review E, Part 2

Key an indented paragraph

Key the paragraph twice DS: once slowly, again at a faster speed.

- Remember to indent.
- Remember to use the CAPS LOCK in line 4 and to strike the LOCK to release the LOCK.

REVIEW E

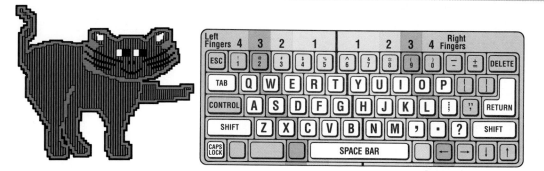

Practice easy phrases (word groups)

```
1  if he|am to|is an|if it|to do|go by
2  an ox|or he|and she|the zoo|she may
3  to do it|is to go|if he is|am to go
```

Practice easy sentences

```
4  I see it is up to me to set a goal.
5  My goal now is to go for good form.
6  I am now on my way to a good speed.
```

Practice an easy paragraph

```
        Go for a goal that is easy to
make at first.  When you make that
rate, move the goal up just a bit:
one or two GWAM at a time.  Try it.
```

**Keyboard review
and mastery**

Key each line twice SS: once slowly,
again at a faster speed. DS below
each 2-line group.

 **GOALS**

- quiet (steady) hands
- elbows steady at your sides
- wrists low, but not touching the
  machine

 PRACTICE HINT

- *Think* and *say* each letter as you
  key it. Keep fingers upright.

 TECHNIQUE HINT

- Reach from bottom row to third row
  (and from third row to bottom row)
  without moving your hands up or
  down the keyboard.

LESSON 19

Keyboard review (all letters used)

1 form word push very flax jerk quite

2 a box a jet an oak the zoo her luck

3 Set a new goal if you wish to grow.

Practice words with side-by-side reaches

4 as oil wet top buy elk ore her open

5 a pot|as her|we buy|has elk|top oil

6 We will try to buy a quart of milk.

Practice words with long reaches

7 my any ice orb sun fun oft bum aqua

8 to my|if any|for ice|the gym|a myth

9 Cey said my unit must set the pace.

Review E, Part 3

Improve keystroking speed on sentences

1. Take a 20-second (20″) timed writing on each sentence. Your rate in gross words a minute (*GWAM*) is shown word for word above the lines.
2. Take another 20″ writing on each line. Try to increase speed.

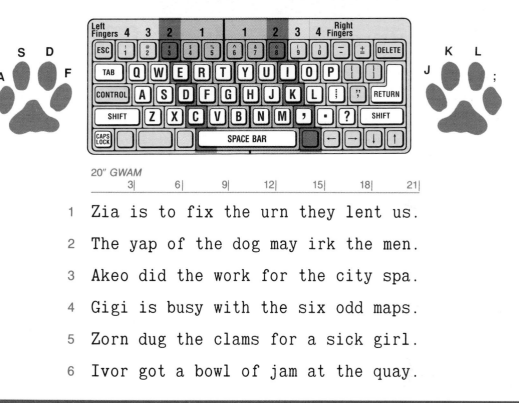

20″ GWAM

3		6		9		12		15		18		21	

1 Zia is to fix the urn they lent us.

2 The yap of the dog may irk the men.

3 Akeo did the work for the city spa.

4 Gigi is busy with the six odd maps.

5 Zorn dug the clams for a sick girl.

6 Ivor got a bowl of jam at the quay.

Review E, Part 4

Measure your keyboarding speed

1. Time yourself to see how long it takes you to key the paragraph.
2. Key the paragraph again. Try to reduce the time to complete it.

Easy paragraph (all letters used)

You may be amazed at just how much you have learned so far. The next goal is right ahead. It will pay you to work on and not to quit.

Lesson 18, Part C

Build keyboarding speed

Key each line twice SS.

 PRACTICE HINT ▶

- *Think, say,* and *key* letter by letter.

 PRACTICE HINT ▶

- *Think, say,* and *key* each word as a word.

PRACTICE HINT ▶

- *Think, say,* and *key* the words shown in color as words. *Think, say,* and *key* the words shown in black letter by letter.

Lesson 18, Part D

Improve keystroking speed on sentences

Take three 15-second (15″) writings on each line. Your rate in gross words a minute (*GWAM*) is shown word by word above the lines.

NOTE: If you finish a line before 15″ are up, start over.

Practice words by *letter* response

```
1  as up we in at on ax no are you see

2  as in|at no|a mop|my sax|we saw him

3  As my dad saw, you were on a barge.
```

Practice words by *word* response

```
4  do is of am it or go me she cut off

5  of it|to us|is he|if she|to own the

6  She is to go to the lake to fix it.
```

Combine *letter* and *word* responses

```
7  do we of ad to my an be the him and

8  to be|if we|to add|of him|is my own

9  He was to see us at the bus at six.
```

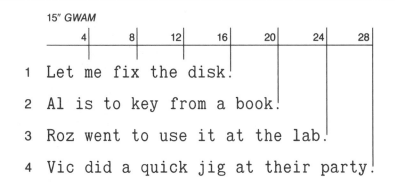

15″ GWAM

```
        4|   8|   12|   16|   20|   24|   28|

1  Let me fix the disk.

2  Al is to key from a book.

3  Roz went to use it at the lab.

4  Vic did a quick jig at their party.
```

UNIT 2

YOU BUILD SKILL ON THE LETTER KEYBOARD

Lessons 16-19

YOUR GOALS

In this unit of 4 lessons, you will:

1. Improve the technique (form) with which you key copy.
2. Improve the speed at which you key copy.
3. Improve the control or accuracy with which you key copy.
4. Increase the number of words that you can key with ease.

LESSON 18

Lesson 18, Part A

Keyboard review and mastery

Key each line twice SS: once slowly, again at a faster speed. DS below each 2-line group.

GOALS ▶

- quiet (steady) hands
- elbows steady at your sides
- wrists low, but not touching the machine

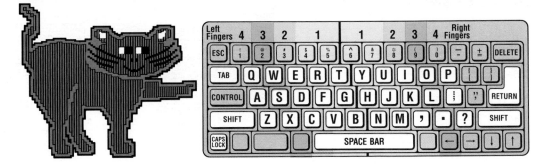

Keyboard review (all letters used)

1 by go me he fix for ale dot sit pay

2 quiz park clam give when next major

3 Is good form the key to high speed?

Lesson 18, Part B

Letter emphasis drill

Each line contains at least 5 uses of the letter shown in color at its left.

1. Key each line once DS.
2. Key again any line(s) that caused you trouble.

Letter emphasis drill

s Signe sang a song on the last show.

t Theo is to go with them to the hut.

u Ula put a fur rug under a blue urn.

v Vic drove the mauve van five miles.

w Will new laws make owners owe more?

x Xica will fix the next axle by six.

y Yoko left for your city by bicycle.

z Zahn plays lazy jazz in the piazza.

Lesson 16, Part A

Keyboard review and mastery

Key each line twice SS: once slowly, again at a faster speed. DS below each 2-line group.

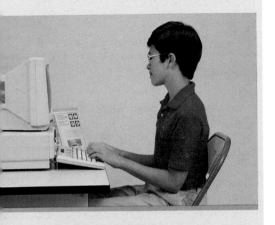

Lesson 16, Part B

Letter emphasis drill

Each line contains at least 5 uses of the letter shown in color at its left.

1. Key each line once DS.
2. Key again any line(s) that caused you trouble.

LESSON 16

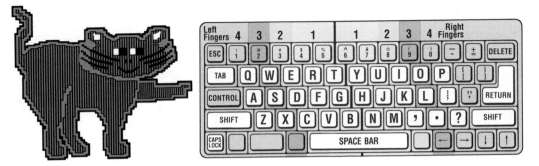

Reach review (all reaches learned)

1 rf uj ed ik ws ol qa p; gf hj za ?;

2 xs .l cd ,k vf mj bf nj tf yj :; fj

3 old kid zap den sow jug six big cud

Letter emphasis drill

a Alan ate a big apple and an orange.

b Bev went by the buoy in a big boat.

c Cliff can pack the coins in a sack.

d Dodi went down to the old oak dock.

e Elvin can see the need to be quick.

f Fuji had felt fine before she fell.

g Gordy is to get a gold nugget ring.

h Heidi hit her head on an old shelf.

i Ivan likes living on the big river.

Lesson 17, Part C

Review spacing with punctuation

Key each line twice SS; DS below each 2-line group.

RECALL ▼

- Space twice after end-of-sentence punctuation marks (. and ?)
- Space once after within-sentence marks ; and , but twice after :
- Space once after . at end of initial or abbreviation

Lesson 17, Part D

Build keyboarding speed

1. Take two 20-second (20") timed writings on each line. If you finish a line before time is called, start over. *GWAM* is shown word by word.

 **GOAL** ▶

- To finish keying the line just as time is called.

2. Take two 1-minute (1') timed writings on the paragraph. See how many words you can key in a minute.

To find *GWAM:* Read the nearest number (or dot) above the point at which you stopped.

Spacing with punctuation marks

1 Is it Jay? I know it is; he spoke.

2 Major, my dog, has gone to the vet.

3 Key these names: Ed, Jo, and Troy.

4 Ms. Isobe said B. J. won the prize.

5 Use i.e. for that is; ft. for feet.

Sentence timed writing

20" GWAM

| | 3| | 6| | 9| | 12| | 15| | 18| | 21| |

1 The town is to pay me for the sign.

2 She is to go to the firm with them.

3 Pam saw the man peek into the auto.

4 See if the girls are in their pool.

Paragraph timed writing (all letters used)

.   2   .   4   .   6
    Next you can learn to work on

.   8   .   10   .   12
the figure bank. Seize the chance

14   .   16   .   18   .   20
to move up in skill. The job will

.   22   .   24   .   26   .
not be simple, but do not quit yet.

Lesson 16, Part C

Improve keyboarding technique

Key each line twice SS.

 PRACTICE HINT ▶

- *Think, say,* and *key* the words at a brisk pace; space quickly.

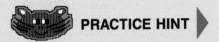 **PRACTICE HINT** ▶

- Shift, strike the key, and release both in a 1-2-3 count.

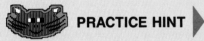 **PRACTICE HINT** ▶

- Keep up your pace to the end of the line, return quickly, and start the next line without a pause.

Lesson 16, Part D

Build keyboarding speed

1. Take a 20-second (20″) timed writing on each line. If you finish a line before time is called, start over. *GWAM* is shown word by word.
2. Do the lines again.

 **GOAL** ▶

- To finish keying the line just as time is called.

Space bar (Use a down-and-in motion.)

```
1  am an by so it ah or of do me to go

2  I am|in it|to me|if so|is an|by the

3  Kent is to go to the zoo with Mala.
```

Shift keys (Shift; strike key; release both.)

```
4  Labor Day|Joji or Aida|April or May

5  Pam and Zoe will play Hal and Theo.

6  May we go with Evan, Jae, and Rosa?
```

Return (Finish line; return; start new line quickly.)

```
7  Xica has set a high goal.

8  Key the names at high speed.

9  Try to key the word with good form.
```

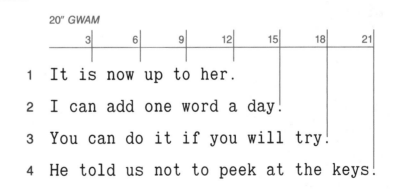

20″ GWAM

	3	6	9	12	15	18	21

```
1  It is now up to her.

2  I can add one word a day.

3  You can do it if you will try.

4  He told us not to peek at the keys.
```

**Keyboard review
and mastery**

Key each line twice SS: once slowly,
again at a faster speed. DS below
each 2-line group.

 **GOALS** ▶

- curved, upright fingers
- finger (not hand) reaches
- quick, snap keystrokes
- down-and-in spacing

Lesson 17, Part B

Letter emphasis drill

Each line contains at least 5 uses of
the letter shown in color at its left.

1. Key each line once DS.
2. Key again any line(s) that caused
   you trouble.

LESSON 17

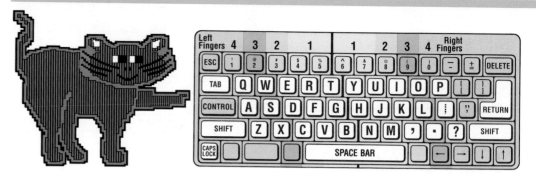

Keyboard review (all letters used)

1 me us if am ox is or it go all dogs

2 by cup jar zoo the van oak wig quit

3 Oki, Al, and Su will go. Will you?

Letter emphasis drill

j Juan just got a job on a major jet.
k Kwan kept skis back of an oak shed.
l Lloyd let her sell a blue jell jar.
m Maria may meet me after math class.
n Nigel will lend a hand when he can.
o Otha took the old book to her room.
p Paul put a pen in his parka pocket.
q Quen quit the squad when Quig quit.
r Rosa ran a torrid race in the rain.